Animals and Why They Matter

Animals
and
Why They Matter

MARY MIDGLEY

WITHDRAWN

The University of Georgia Press
Athens

Copyright © 1983 by Mary Midgley
All rights reserved

Published in 1984 in the United States of America
by the University of Georgia Press, Athens, Georgia 30602.

Printed in the United States of America

Library of Congress Cataloging in Publication Data

Midgley, Mary, 1919–
   Animals and why they matter.

   Includes bibliographical references and index.
   1. Ethics. 2. Social ethics. 3. Social contract.
4. Animals. I. Title.
BJ1012.M5   1984   179′.3   83-17933
ISBN 0-8203-0704-1
ISBN 0-8203-0756-4 (pbk.)

Contents

Foreword

The topic of this book is much bigger than it may seem. It bears on many central themes of political and general philosophy. The animal question has been rather neglected by philosophers till quite lately. But when you really begin to look into it, it raises a host of large and interesting questions about such things as the meaning of equality, the importance of reason in human life and its relation to feeling, the significance of a social contract, the importance of language, the concepts of childhood and maturity, and the human race's general view of itself in relation to the physical universe. Our tradition of thought has, I think, left a surprising gap here. This has damaged our reasoning right across this alarming range of subjects, which are, in anybody's view, extremely important.

Because of their importance, I have kept this book quite untechnical. It is written for the general reader. But because past errors and confusions play so large a part in forming our present attitudes, I have also said a great deal about past controversies. In particular, I have looked at the way in which social-contract thinking, from Hobbes on, has shaped our moral and political ideas, and at the problems this raises, not only about animals, but about women, slaves, aliens and other beings suspected of not being proper contractors. I hope my readers will find this as absorbing as I have. But it has set a certain problem of method. If I had cited references for everything, notes would have swamped my text. As it is, there will certainly be too many notes for some people and too few for others. But I don't think there is anything I can do about that.

A note seems called for about the word *animal*. I have used it throughout, in the way in which it is normally used, to mean animals of other species than man. I have not repeated the point, which I and others have already made, that human beings are themselves animals, rather than vegetables, minerals, angels or fairies, and that this rather odd use of the word sometimes compounds confusions about their actual status. This small matter will, I hope, fall into place in the context of my argument; it has not seemed worthwhile using other phrases throughout.

I would like to thank my friends and colleagues at Newcastle University for a great deal of help and encouragement and Moira Dearden for typing faultlessly an often almost inscrutable text.

1 Getting Animals in Focus

A sense of unreality often blocks our attempts to understand our moral relations with animals. The whole question is hard to fit into our ethical system. Arguments for taking it seriously tend to be dismissed rather than met, to be stigmatized wholesale as perverse, sentimental, emotive, childish, impractical, superstitious, insincere – somehow not solid. They do not, however, go away; if anything, they become more pressing. Now this kind of upsetting clash always deserves serious attention. The first thing to be said about such clashes is that they arise on plenty of other topics as well as about animals. We get a similar unnerving sense of double vision, of hovering between dream and reality, whenever we are confronted with any unsatisfactory and difficult corner of our moral scene. It happens both when principles collide, and when principle merely collides violently with practice. Ethics is practical. If standards conflict, or if they are so high and so general that we cannot see easily how we could act on them, we feel dazed. Still more, if it seems that what we ought to do is something that no reasonable person would consider doing, we get sceptical; we suspect fantasy and confusion. We know that morality does actually need remote and general standards, and must sometimes demand actions which no reasonable person at the time would consider. We know that a morality which never shocks anybody dwindles into etiquette. The history of past reforms, like the abolition of slavery, shows this. All the same, ideals which nobody can translate into action are wasted. This tension is a quite general difficulty of life. (To look at it another way, it is a general factor in making life interesting.) In trying to embody remote general ideals – freedom, equality, love – in what we must hastily do under deplorable conditions at a particular time, we have to work out subsidiary, detailed principles of interpretation. These commonly give us much more trouble than the general and remote ones, because they involve clashes which are simply invisible from the prophetic distance.

I mention this general problem in order to point out that the animal issue is not really an isolated one. It is an aspect of morality like any other. Actually, by working on it, we shall find useful insights which can help us over everyday issues which everybody recognizes to be central.

Many people, however, do have a sense that animals are not a serious case at all, but fall outside the province of morality altogether. They are inclined to endorse Spinoza's view of the matter. Spinoza said:

It is plain that the law against the slaughtering of animals is founded rather on vain superstition and womanish pity than on sound reason. The rational quest of what is useful to us further teaches us the necessity of associating ourselves with our fellow-men, but not with beasts, or things, whose nature is different from our own; we have the same rights in respect of them as they have in respect of us. Nay, as everyone's right is defined by his virtue, or power, men have far greater rights over beasts than beasts have over men. Still, I do not deny that beasts feel; what I deny is, that we may not consult our own advantage and use them as we please, treating them in the way which best suits us; for their nature is not like ours, and their emotions are naturally different from human emotions.[1]

Or, in more modern terms, in an American television programme in 1974:

Robert Nozick asked the scientists whether the fact that an experiment will kill hundreds of animals is ever regarded by scientists as a reason for not performing it. One of the scientists answered, 'Not that I know of'; Nozick pressed his question: 'Don't the animals count at all?' Dr A. Perachio, of the Yerkes centre, replied, 'Why should they?' while Dr D. Baltimore, of the Massachusetts Institute of Technology, added that he did not think that experimenting on animals raised a moral issue at all.[2]

On this view, claims on behalf of animals are not just excessive, but downright nonsensical, as meaningless as claims on behalf of stones or machines or plastic dolls. Others however – and indeed often the same people at different times – feel the force of these claims strongly. Now the sources of this violent clash and confusion are plain enough. There has simply been very little serious thought given to the matter. The hard work of bringing the extreme positions together and hammering sense out of them has never been done. In the West, both the religious and the secular moral traditions have, till lately, scarcely attended to any non-human species. As regards religion, in spite of a few exceptions like St Francis, the main official Christian doctrine has simply excluded animals from consideration as not having souls. It has stressed the Old Testament pronouncements which gave them completely into the power of man as mere instruments for his purposes, and ignored the quite numerous texts which required a different attitude.[3] As for secular thought, this, since the Renaissance, has largely been 'human-ist' in one sense or another, sometimes even in the very strong sense of putting man in the place of God, as Auguste Comte did in his Religion of Humanity. A move like this naturally makes it hard to see that man might have any significant link with other species. Not everybody, of course, went so far as Comte. But enthusiasm for the Rights of Man was usually seen, until quite lately, as fixing the limits of morality to the species barrier.

2 THE EXALTATION OF REASON

Some central Enlightenment thinkers (notably Montaigne, Tom Paine, Voltaire, Bentham and Mill) rejected this idea strongly, and insisted on extending humane consideration to animals. But Enlightenment thought in general was drawn the other way by its exaltation of Reason. If animals are irrational, and value and dignity depend entirely on reason, animals cannot matter. Reason plays the same role here that the soul does in Christian thought. The extreme form of this rationalist view was that of Descartes, who identified the human soul or consciousness so completely with reason as to conclude that animals could not be conscious at all, and were in fact just automata.[4] One can still occasionally find scientists who profess this view, and it is of course the ideal position from which to argue that animals do not matter; it settles the issue at once. To hold it consistently today, however, requires some awkward intellectual gymnastics. In the first place, we now know a great deal more than Descartes did about the brains and nervous systems of our own and other species. If a change so immense as the sudden intrusion of consciousness had taken place at this point, a radical difference ought to be visible here. Of course there are important differences, but they are not on anything like the kind of scale which this suggestion would demand. So it becomes reasonable to ask the question which Voltaire put to the vivisector – 'You discover in it all the same organs of feeling that are in yourself. Answer me, mechanist, has nature arranged all the means of feeling in this animal so that it may not feel?'[5] In the second place, one can scarcely take Descartes' view of animals without accepting also his view of man, which is highly eccentric. It is that a person himself is simply his reason or intellect – the part of him which is not shared with animals. This involves a startling moral position – namely, that nothing non-intellectual really matters.

What has happened to the feelings? Now rationalistic moralists who have thought like this, such as Plato and Spinoza, have in fact always included in 'reason' a great deal more than mere intellect. They have meant by 'reason' a contemplative faculty, an insight into values, and also a willingness to respond to them, including, effectively, the love of the good. But this, most people would now suppose, involves an emotional element as well as an intellectual one. Mind and heart do not make sense apart, and the heart is something which, on the face of it, we share with animals. The common view today would probably be that, roughly speaking, people have the faculties which animals have, with some unique and crucial additions. Again, most people today, if asked whether they think that man is essentially a rational being, will reply confidently that they don't think he is rational at all. This remark has to be something of an exaggeration. But it conveys a strong current conviction that the Enlightenment's exaltation of the intellect as the core of human life was excessive, and needs to be corrected.

This seems to be right. The exaggeration was in its time a useful and entirely justifiable one, in view of the irrational prejudices which had to be fought, both in politics and in the development of science. But such exaggerations have to be dropped when they have served their purpose and begin to do harm. I cannot here go properly into the complex problems which arise about the relation of reason to feeling. I shall say some more about them in Chapter 3.[6] My point now is simply that the rationalist tradition did in general, as much as the Christian one, dismiss animals out of hand from the moral scene, that it did so on grounds that are not obviously acceptable today, and that the subject did, therefore, largely escape attention. Two other developments have since helped to obscure it further. First, the industrial revolution moved most of us into towns, and replaced horses by machines. There had always been a tendency for scholars to be town-dwellers, but it now increased, and towns became almost cleared of animals. Out of sight accordingly became out of mind. (Compare the effect of secluding women in a harem.) Secondly, morality itself, as directed towards people, became more ambitious. A thousand evils which had seemed inevitable in the eighteenth century, from cholera and tuberculosis to low wages and capital punishment for theft, were dragged into the area of responsibility and treated as things to be remedied. Tremendous work was done on these things during the last century and has continued since. But it still sometimes seems as if the problems never grow less.

3   ABSOLUTE AND RELATIVE DISMISSAL

The gap between humanitarian ideals and actual social practice remains enormous. It is not surprising that some people, concentrating on that gap, brush aside claims made on behalf of animals as a mere distraction. This certainly has been a factor in making them seem unreal. But here the reasons for dismissing them are quite different. Humanitarians occupied with human problems do not usually dismiss animal claims as just nonsensical, like claims on behalf of stones. Instead, they merely give them a very low priority. The suggestion is now that animals, since they are conscious, are entitled to *some* consideration, but must come at the end of the queue, after all human needs have been met. I shall call this idea relative dismissal or low priority, to distinguish it from absolute dismissal. As we shall see, the distinction makes a good deal of difference in practice, since many claims on behalf of animals do not compete with real human needs at all, and therefore do not seem to stand in the same queue. Englishmen baiting bears were not in the same position as Eskimoes killing them in self-defence. But the point to notice now about this argument is simply that it *is* different. Our mental vertigo comes from confusing many different positions. Disentangling them is the path to relief.

4 THE RETURN OF THE ANIMALS

Different as they are, however, all these lines of thought have converged to discourage attention to animals. At the same time, in another part of the forest, various influences have produced a new and remarkable upsurge of interest in them. The ground was prepared for this by the slow, persistent work of those Enlightenment humanitarians who did care about animals – Bentham, Mill, Shaftesbury, Voltaire, Tom Paine, Shaw and others. From the eighteenth century on, they struggled to mitigate the more savage forms of cruelty. Through their efforts laws were passed, customs altered and permissible treatment of animals brought within much narrower limits. This has certainly had its effect on the way in which animals are thought of. Such work has in general been accepted, even if on somewhat uncertain terms, as included within ordinary morality. But its hold on the public imagination has not been very strong. People in general have perhaps thought of animal welfare as they have thought of drains – as a worthy but not particularly interesting subject. In the last few decades, however, their imagination has been struck, somewhat suddenly, by a flood of new and fascinating information about animals. Some dim conception of splendours and miseries hitherto undreamt of, of the vast range of sentient life, of the richness and complexity found in even the simplest creatures, has started to penetrate even to the least imaginative. For the first time in civilized history, people who were interested in animals because they wanted to understand them, rather than just to eat or yoke or shoot or stuff them, have been able to advance that understanding by scientific means, and to convey some of it to the inquisitive public. Animals have to some extent come off the page. With the bizarre assistance of TV, Darwin is at last getting through. Town-dwellers are beginning to notice the biosphere.

Now this interest is, of course, in the first place a speculative rather than a practical one. It appeals to sheer wonder – in the first place to the gaping eye, which may, obviously, only gape idly and draw no conclusions from what it sees. The travellers' tales which we have long had often led nowhere, because marvels which are reported and received merely as marvels mean little to us. Ethologists, however, are by no means just marvel-hunters. Their first concern is with the *meaning* of behaviour, with sorting out one motivation from another, with understanding how each kind of social life works. In doing this they inevitably find and point out many patterns which resemble those in human life. This is not because they illicitly project human qualities onto animals, but because human life really does have an animal basis – an emotional structure on which we build what is distinctively human. In spite of the differences, quite complex aspects of things like loneliness and play and maternal affection, ambition and rivalry and fear, turn out to be shared with other social creatures. The more we know about their detailed behaviour, the clearer and more interesting this continuity becomes. Accordingly, to grasp more fully how their lives work inevitably gives us a sense of fellowship with them. And at this point an emotional and practical concern does naturally tend to join the speculative one. The more clearly we see the difference between animals and stones or machines or plastic dolls, the less likely it seems that we ought to treat them in the same way. There has undoubtedly been a marked change in the last few decades in the moral view that ordinary people take of these questions, once they are brought to their notice.

5 WHAT DID THE DISMISSERS MEAN?

To bring out this change, I quote here a story about elephant-hunting. It comes from a book published in 1850, but it would, I think, have passed without comment as normal at a much later date. It occurs in the memoirs of one R. Gordon Cummings. He relates first how the Africans do all his stalking for him and lead him up at a suitable angle to the elephant. Then, Cummings writes:

The elephant stood broadside to me, at upwards of one hundred yards, and his attention at the moment was occupied with the dogs ... I fired at his shoulder, and secured him with a single shot. The ball caught him high on the shoulder-blade, rendering him instantly dead lame; and before the echo of the bullet could reach my ear, I plainly saw the elephant was mine . . . I resolved to devote a short time to the contemplation of this noble elephant before laying him low; accordingly, having off-saddled the horses beneath a shady tree, which was to be my quarters for the night and the ensuing day, I quickly kindled a fire and put on the kettle, and in a very few minutes my coffee was prepared. There I sat in my forest home, coolly sipping my coffee, with one of the finest elephants in Africa awaiting my pleasure beside a neighbouring tree. It was indeed a striking scene; and as I gazed upon the stupendous veteran of the' forest, I thought of the red deer which I loved to follow in my native land, and felt that, though fates had driven me to follow a more daring and arduous avocation in a distant land, it was a good exchange that I had made, for I was now a chief over boundless forests, which yielded unspeakably more noble and exciting sport.

Having admired the elephant for a considerable time, I resolved to make experiments for vulnerable points . . . [He bungles this again and again; eventually, after even he has become a little worried, he succeeds in wounding the elephant fatally.] Large tears now trickled from his eyes, which he slowly shut and opened, his colossal frame quivered convulsively, and, falling on his side, he expired. The tusks of this elephant were beautifully arched, and were the heaviest I had yet met with, averaging 90 pounds weight apiece.[7]

I do not know whether there are still old gentlemen around today who can cheerfully look at that episode exactly as Cummings did, as a piece of perfectly natural civilized behaviour. There are plenty of records to show how freely this was done, notably the many photographs – taken regularly after a successful day's shooting – which show King Edward VII and similar heroes standing on lawns besides mountains of dead deer and birds. For most of us, however, the light seems somehow to have changed – indeed, it probably did so during the First World War. We cannot see things that way any longer.

At this point I think it would be useful if readers who are feeling fairly dismissive about animal claims would use Cummings's case as a test to decide whether their dismissal is actually relative or absolute. For an absolute dismisser, there is nothing wrong with Cummings's conduct at all, and could not be whatever further refinements he might have added, so long as they damaged nobody but the elephant. Here some interesting considerations come in, because this test is not completely simple to apply. Other faults usually do accompany such cases, and they may be held to damage the human agent himself independently of damage to the animal. Cummings, for instance, shows glaring faults of confused vainglory and self-deception ('awaiting my pleasure . . . a chief over boundless forests'). These may be held to degrade him simply as a human being. As it happens, too, rationalists are particularly sensitive to such faults. It may be suggested also that treating animals like this might, though harmless in itself, have bad consequences in making people callous in their treatment of human beings. Kant, indeed, thought that this dangerous effect was the only thing necessarily wrong about ill-treating animals.[8] Taking this sort of view, an absolute dismisser might condemn Cummings for self-deception, damage to his own moral potentialities and perhaps bad taste, but still say that he did so without conceding that it mattered at all what was done to the elephant.

6   THE MEANING OF ELEPHANTICIDE

It is not clear, however, that this distinction will work. These internal faults in the hunter cannot be separated from an actual offence against the animal; they only make sense if that outward injury is admitted. The self-deception indeed is real enough. It flows from a false view of one's own achievements, in particular of what can be considered as achieved by shooting game. It is not possible to become a ruler, entitled to fantasies of empire and dominion, simply by letting off guns. These fantasies, however, are not misleading in their central implication that the elephant is conscious, and in some sense a worthy adversary. That is essential to them. Sane people do not usually congratulate themselves in this way if they have merely smashed a machine or a plastic toy, or even blown up an enormous boulder. They choose a large animal because they can think of it, not just as an obstacle, but as an *opponent* – a being like themselves in having its own emotions and interest. Other similar sports make this plain. Bull-baiting has not been replaced by bulldozer-baiting, because active personal conflict is essential to such affairs. The self-deception of hunters like Cummings seems therefore to be of the same kind which is found in a murderer who supposes that by shooting an opponent from behind a hedge he has proved himself superior to his victim. It is not like that involved in smashing a machine because one thinks it is attacking one. It depends on a true belief in the consciousness, complexity and independence of the victim, accompanied by a false estimate of what is achieved by killing him. But the main fault, in both cases, depends on the true belief, not on the false one. The viciousness of the false thought is derivative. Crude complacency is indeed an aggravation of homicide, but it only becomes a terrible fault in itself if the homicide is so in the first place. The same seems true for elephanticide. As for the danger of becoming callous towards people by being so towards elephants, that too seems only to arise if the two kinds of case are seen as essentially similar, even if different in degree. A mechanic who is trained in taking cars to pieces is not thought likely to drift insensibly as a result of his work into taking people to pieces as well, nor would this excuse cut much ice if he did so. He is supposed to know the difference. And accordingly, taking cars to pieces is not even viewed as bad taste.

7 THE OBSCURITY OF ABSOLUTE DISMISSAL

It is worth going into all this because (as I believe) it may emerge that a position of absolute dismissal is oftener professed than held. It is more obscure, and harder to maintain, than it at first appears. To think of a being as conscious does, for most of us, involve thinking that it has some value in itself, that it matters. And about the treatment of animals, most people do in fact draw the line somewhere. To torment, for no good reason, a creature which is captive and helpless – even, like Cummings, to torment it simply by delay – does seem to most people objectionable in itself, quite apart from self-deception and corrupting effects. Children (for instance) caught doing such things are not usually allowed to continue. This means that, however far down the queue animals may be placed, it is still possible in principle for their urgent needs to take precedence over people's trivial ones. The dismissal is then only partial and relative. This will become important in Chapter 4, where we shall consider explicit philosophical arguments for absolute dismissal. Throughout this book, however, I shall go on taking absolute dismissal seriously because, though few people now maintain this attitude consistently, very many fall back on it occasionally, viewing it as a safe logical refuge in awkward cases. Someone who is considerate on principle to his pets, and even actively concerned about wild life, may still think that the question simply does not arise whether he should have any scruples about hurting experimental animals, or eating factory-farmed meat, or even hunting. I am not of course saying that this sort of position cannot be justified, simply that it seems on the face of things to need justifying, and the absolute dismisser thinks all argument irrelevant. He takes the exclusion of animals from serious concern as something obvious and established. Against that background, any sympathy or regard that we may choose to pay to some of them counts as something of an optional fancy, not any sort of a duty. And the habit of dismissal is indeed solid and established, but the arguments for it are quite another matter. In fact, as commonly happens where arguments are invented to justify a position which is not really questioned, because it is already habitual and appeals to self-interest, these arguments are an unimpressive lot, and they have been getting increasingly out of kilter with the rest of our thinking. Many of them have consequences which, when they are pointed out, scarcely anybody is likely to welcome today. Nor are they needed to enable the human race to get on with its own concerns in a sensible and efficient manner. In short, the arguments for absolute dismissal are an incubus, a dead weight on our thinking, which should be studied because we need to get rid of it, and which distorts our ideas on many subjects apparently remote from the present one. In this chapter, we have simply pointed out the confusion to which it contributes – the dilemma which arises in a culture habituated to ignoring the interests of animals, when a Darwinian and humanitarian perspective is introduced, which shows them as important in their own right. In the next chapter we will look at one simple way of by-passing that dilemma.

2 *Competition is Real but Limited*

I THE LIFEBOAT MODEL

The problem of competition presents itself to many people in a form more or less like this: Must we really acknowledge all our long-lost cousins and heave them into the humanitarian lifeboat, which is already foundering under the human race? Or can we take another look at the rule-book and declare the relationship too distant, so that we are justified in letting the whole lot sink?

In this form, the dilemma is extremely alarming, and it is not surprising that those who perceive it in this way don't want to look at it very often. In Chapters 4 and 6 we will consider these extreme solutions (in the reverse order). Both have obvious attractions, notably in simplicity. Both do contain important parts of the truth. But both (as I shall suggest) share a common fault of unreality and excessive abstraction, a fault which vitiates their views of human life before we ever reach the question of animals. Each attempts to standardize our moral relations to our fellow-beings around a single simple model. Our social capacities are much too complex to allow of this. We naturally respond to various fellow-beings in various ways. This is crucial both within our own species and outside it. Our social life, our interests and our sympathy both can and must extend outside our own species, but they do so with a difference. Animals, too, are not just 'animals'. They are elephants or amoebae, locusts or fish or deer. In later chapters I shall consider the effect of these various differences on two quite distinct sorts of moral claim that may arise on behalf of animals – social claims (on behalf of individual creatures) and ecological claims (on behalf of whole populations and species). A more sensitive and realistic approach to the species-barrier will, I believe, show both sorts of claim as real, though not (any more than any other sort of moral claim) necessarily bound to prevail in a particular situation of conflict.

The two solutions just mentioned are, however, extreme views, programmes of absolute dismissal and absolute inclusion. They are drastic responses to the lifeboat dilemma which we are now considering. Now that dilemma itself does not in principle demand a drastic response.

It claims to be merely competitive and economic, arguing simply from shortage of resources. There is not (it says) enough of everything for human beings. If there were enough, it might (it concedes) be nice to give something to animals too. As things are, however (it regretfully concludes), they must get either everything or nothing, and the reasonable answer is nothing. In the present chapter, then, we had better look, briefly but sharply, at the lifeboat model. This model, as we see at once, is no stranger. It is in very common use, not to protect, but to attack, the claims of those crowds of needy, distant human beings whom it here seems to champion against animals.[1] In fact – to come to the point at once – this model is an inadequate one for most of the situations where it is applied to human affairs.

It often militates against generosity, justice, intelligent invention and even enlightened self-interest. It tends to generate bad faith. The point is that we are not usually in lifeboats. In a lifeboat (at least in a completely full one) there is no choice available but one, and fellow-beings can present themselves to the boaters in one capacity only – as 'possible beneficiaries',[2] which is to say (expressed more darkly) as competitors for a few fixed, unexpandable resources. I am tempted to say that life is *never* like this. That would be an exaggeration, but the exaggeration usually goes so monstrously the other way that it is worth making. Lifeboat situations are supposed to be ones in which our ingenuity can do *nothing*, either to increase existing resources or to distribute them better. (Boats cannot be redistributed, which is why they are often chosen for such arguments.) It is not clear, however, how anyone could ever be sure that he had exhausted the resources of possible thinking. Most commonly we have not even tried to use them. Even on the raft of the *Medusa*, resources of kindness and good-will were available, which would at least have made dying easier, and might possibly have organized a rescue. A recent Oxfam pamphlet answered lifeboat-style objections to international aid by remarking that 10 per cent of the world's population now consumes 90 per cent of its resources. Whatever sort of a situation that may be, it does not seem to be a lifeboat one for the 10 per cent. Yet it can quite easily appear so, if once one fastens one's mind exclusively on competition. The point that needs to be raised about 'possible beneficiaries' is that nearly all such people (in life, as opposed to imaginary lifeboats) are not only competitors, but also possible allies, friends and helpers, on whom our wider interests may at any time depend. It is a confused notion of prudence which treats them simply as blind mouths, and limits self-interest to the purely defensive business of hanging on to our existing resources. Using those resources to make friends is in general a far better investment. In the end, we are all in the same boat.

My point here is obviously not a high-minded but a crudely prudential one. (I am putting more exalted considerations aside for the minute to meet the objector on his own ground.) Competition is *not* the basic law of life. No social group is ever so isolated and so independent that it can write off the disasters, and the possible resentment, of everybody outside it. Images of lifeboats must be corrected here by more relevant ones of cholera and oppression. We are incurably members one of another. This point has become a trifle hard to see lately because liberal political theory, for good reasons, has tended to stress the isolation of every rational subject and his right to choose his own political links and affiliations. In many situations this is a proper and vital corrective. But it is misleading to exaggerate it into a kind of universal social chemistry, an atomic theory proving that every individual is originally distinct, and needs some special reason if he is to connect himself with any other.[3] The presumption is the other way. We are indeed individuals, but ones who could not exist if we had not been brought up in groups, and when those groups set themselves one against another, a reason must be given for that.

There are, of course, real and very difficult questions about how wide we shall take our group to be, and how, at each stage, we shall arrange to arbitrate between it and its neighbours. Within the human race, competition is real, and has always been troublesome to deal with. The lifeboat model, however, is objectionable because it excuses us from dealing with these problems at all. It draws a sharp line at which efforts at further detailed negotiation are simply going to stop. Trevor Huddleston has said that the proverb 'charity begins at home' is perhaps the most disastrous saying ever coined. This is not because of its literal meaning, but because of the unspoken thought which usually goes with it – namely, that it ought to end there too. The proverb makes two points, of which the first is uncontroversial. This is that our powers actually are limited. Competition in general is real (though, of course, it still may not be so in any particular case). The second point is that those nearest to us have special claims on those limited powers – claims which diminish in proportion to distance. If, therefore, these were the only claims we knew of, then the most distant (physically or socially) must always come at the end of the queue. This principle of nearness or kinship has been used to defend a wide variety of behaviour which can loosely be called selfish, from the dismissal of animals now under discussion through various forms of political narrowness right up to egoism proper, which admits no claims except one's own. I shall argue throughout this book that the proper way to treat it is to recognize nearness as a perfectly real and important factor in our psychology, and therefore in our morality, but to refuse to treat it as the sole or supreme one. We are subject to other claims. Nearness alone can never have a walkover.

2   HOW MUCH DOES KINSHIP MATTER?

Many reformers, however, have wanted to go much further than this, and to root out altogether this whole notion of claims conferred simply by social nearness and particularly by kinship. Most notably, Plato tried to get rid of them from the lives of the Guardians in his *Republic*.[4] These people ought, he says, always to say *mine* and *yours* in unison and not in competition. They must, therefore, have nothing identifiable as their own, not even their own parents and children. Some modern feminists have made similar drastic proposals, rejecting the whole notion of nearness or belonging as artificial, a mere confusion introduced by bad cultures.[5] In what sense something fundamental to, and valued by, all existing cultures can be so dismissed is not clear. (It may be all right to say that one is introducing, positively, a new human value which has not yet been seen. But to reject – destructively – a universal existing value seems rather arrogant.)

It is worth noticing that those who have made any attempt in practice to introduce this sort of institution have by no means abandoned the notion of nearness, but have merely shifted it for defensive reasons to a slightly wider margin. The Spartan ruling class, which was Plato's chief model, did indeed make great and successful efforts to weaken the claims of family on its members. But it did so in order to strengthen their loyalty to their class, a small group united in a permanent state of suspicious hostility to the much more numerous serfs on whom they depended. Plato himself conceived his citizens as commuting personal claims into loyalty to the Republic itself, which would need defence against outside attackers, as well as against corruption. Similar consider-ations have weighed with the state of Israel. Even monastic institutions, which are not warlike, consider strict brotherhood or sisterhood as holding only within the order, and the community itself is an essential unit for them. All these are special cases, and it is rare for such experiments to have any success at all. I do not think that any case has been made out for supposing that people are capable of being emotionally impartial (other than by having all their emotions stunted), nor for denying that closeness imposes special duties. But this in itself is not morally alarming, because we have other duties (notably those deriving from justice and compassion) which, when strong, can outweigh those we owe to the people immediately around us.

The moral universe is not just a system of concentric circles, in which inner claims must always prevail over outer ones. The source of trouble does not really lie in learning to say *mine* and *yours* normally, nor in admitting the claims of *mine*, but in failing to make the next move – one which is obvious and very important in the development of children – towards grasping the claims of *yours* and learning how conflicts can be arbitrated. The Good Samaritan helped the injured stranger, because he recognized a serious emergency, making a strong claim of its own whoever it belonged to. In doing this, as Christ remarked, he acted *as a neighbour* to him who fell among thieves. The Samaritan is not a man brought up to be above such notions as *neighbourhood*, nor one who thinks that everybody is always his neighbour. He is one who has understood this idea so fully that he knows how, on occasion, to extend it. Nearly everybody recognizes a similar principle over natural disasters like earthquakes, and most cultures contain rules prescribing special duties to such classes as strangers, suppliants, lunatics and the like. The difficulty lies just in the inflexibility of these rules, and in a tendency for the easily felt, habitual claims of nearness to override them. But this is a very different thing from a general law saying that nearness must always prevail.

I am suggesting that – contrary to the views of some egalitarians – those who use the lifeboat model are right to suppose that, in cases of real, sharp, life-or-death competition, we can indeed owe special, overriding duties based on kinship and other forms of social nearness. From a burning building, or even a milder disaster, we are right to rescue first our nearest and dearest. Theorists who deny this, exalting impartiality as the core of virtue, are muddled. And this is true of nearness in species as well as of other kinds. But it cannot possibly mean that those further from us are always too far down the queue to be reached. There are two reasons for this. First, sharp competition is not always present. (In fact, for us in the prosperous West it is pretty rare.) And second, there are plenty of other claims which can, on occasion, outweigh nearness.

Many people will, no doubt, accept this argument in a general way so far as it applies to the human race, but will think that it cannot reach beyond the species barrier. Why not? If we are still thinking of competition, of relative dismissal, the difficulty seems to be one of fixing, so to speak, the inter-species exchange rate. I have suggested – and my readers must decide the case for themselves – that confronted with Cummings and his gun, we might consider that the elephant's life, along with the conditions of its last hour, ought to outweigh the hunter's foolish pleasure in self-glorification, even when the profit on the tusks is thrown in. (If this is not accepted, we can take even stronger cases.) The point to be noticed is this. If the exchange rate is placed so favourably to the human race that competition must virtually always be decided in our favour, then relative dismissal declines into absolute dismissal. Is there any reason why it should do this?

3 NATURE IS NOT ALWAYS RED IN TOOTH AND CLAW

There exists, I believe, an impression that it must do so because of the working of natural selection – that cut-throat competition between species is the law of evolution. This is false, and the reading of such pop-gun fantasies into evolutionary theory is a serious error. We had better look into the matter. The first thing to be said is that the competition relevant to natural selection is mainly that within a species, rather than that without. It is within each species that the selection of different lines produces changes. The second thing to say is that competition, in the vast, impersonal sense required for talking about evolution, goes on, both within species and between them, without the consciousness of those involved in it, and does not at all require what we think of on our tiny scale as deliberate competitive behaviour. (Indeed, it is often best tackled by friendliness and co-operation.) In that vast, impersonal sense, creatures are 'in competition' if they use the same limited resources, and the competition is keen in proportion to the limitation. This means that, with keen competition, if nothing else changes, one of any two competing species will eventually vanish. But very often something else does change.

A species in such a situation does not at all need to proceed by aggressively grabbing more of the contested resource. It often survives by 'learning' to use something different, or to make better use of what it has got – for instance by a more efficient digestive system, or (like desert creatures) by a more productive use of water. Moreover, it would be quite false to say that competition is the only relation that obtains between species. Mutual dependence is in general quite as important. Each kind exists within an ecosystem, and needs the others to keep the system going. Thus, grazing animals on the African plains co-exist because each specializes in eating some particular kind of plant, and needs the others to keep the whole pasture at a balanced level. They depend, too, on each other's specialized capacities to give warning of danger. We shall discuss later the extent to which conscious, social relations between species are added to this.[6] It is slight but real. Beyond this, and quite impersonally, each also depends for survival on innumerable others, such as the insects which pollinate the plants, the fauna of their intestines and of course their predators. It is unthinkable that any species should be an island.

It used, I think, to be assumed that people stood outside this system and could ignore it, because they were culturally so flexible and could live anywhere. In the last few decades we have found out the hard way how wrong this was. Insecticides and the like, thrust slapdash into complex ecosystems, have produced disasters by killing, along with our competitors, squadrons of our friends and allies of whom we were entirely unaware. People supposed that all they had to do to increase resources was to destroy their competitors – insect pests, rodents and others – and walk away with the proceeds. Had competition actually been the basic law of life, they ought to have been right. But they weren't. Things have therefore gone badly wrong. On a wide ecological scale, human resource use is typically moving from a fairly stable arrangement to one where small groups of human beings are destroying, for short-term profit, habitats which the entire human race need as badly as the local fauna, and which, if better managed, would easily support all of them. This is as true of dust-bowl farming in the USA as of tropical forests, and it is happening to some extent everywhere. In such cases, to concentrate on the animals as competitors is dangerously misleading. Other noticeable species – elephants, apes, deer, tigers, birds – are hardly ever decisive competitors. They are primarily fellow-sufferers and useful indicators of shared trouble. The competition that kills is – as usual – within the species. Competitive pressure, therefore, will scarcely provide a wholesale justification for taking it out on outsiders. Unrestrained competition is the law, not of life, but of death.

To sum up so far: The point of this chapter has been to discuss the idea that pressures of competition can settle out of hand all questions about our relation to animals – that our interests are so sharply threatened that any consideration for outsiders is a non-starter. I have suggested that this is, on the whole, false, and is as plainly so over animals as over our own species. The claims of those nearest to us are real, but they cannot automatically override those of the more distant, unless a special urgency is shown to force that decision. About animals, much of the time there is no such urgency. The spectrum of animal use stretches right from the Eskimo defending himself, through pest control, medical research, roast lamb, fox-hunting, pâté de foie gras, the use of sperm whale oil when satisfactory substitutes are already available, LD 50 testing, on to Cummings with his gun and beyond that to further reaches too offensive to mention. The plea of severe competitive pressure is not going to hold much beyond the first four items, if so far.

4 THE REALITY OF CONFLICT

It is important here however to concede that those first items do pose real problems. I do not at all want to deny this. There are cases where competition between people and other species is unavoidable and drastic. Meat-eating, if we take it to be necessary, is one of them, but it does not stand alone and ought not to be made the decisive issue. Crop pests of all kinds – not just insects, but rodents, birds, even deer, baboons and elephants – *must* be killed, if only by starvation, by people who mean to survive, and this would be true even in a world of Jains.

The same is true, still more obviously, of disease bacilli and parasites – a feature of life not noticed when the Jain philosophy was developed. Zoophiles have, I think, sometimes weakened their case by being too off-hand about all this – by talking as if vegetarianism settled all the problems of competition. They have also made things extremely hard for themselves lately by talking in a very wholesale, *a priori*, French-revolutionary sort of way about all animals being equal, and denouncing 'speciesism' as being an irrational form of discrimination, comparable to racism. This way of thinking is hard to apply convincingly to locusts, hookworms and spirochaetes, and was invented without much attention to them. (We shall discuss these problems in Chapters 6 to 9.) My point at the moment is simply that discrimination – meaning the power of distinguishing intelligently between different kinds of cases – is absolutely essential for the whole issue. We can no more think sensibly about our duties to animals-in-general than to human-beings-in-general. The device of invoking competition in order to lump them all together will not work. Our actual competitive relations with various sorts of animals differ enormously. And relations of other kinds can always be more important than competitive ones. The obsession with competition alone is as distorting outside our own species as within it.

It should be noticed, moreover, that competition, while it may give a licence to kill, does not on its own seem to give also a licence for what may be called refinements to the process. An elephant killed for strictly competitive reasons – for necessary meat, or to save crops – ought not to be kept waiting, half-killed, while those in charge have their coffee. This view would, I think, be accepted by most reasonably humane people today – once the point was brought to their notice. It has, however, some quite important immediate consequences which have not yet come to their notice enough, about such things as the treatment of animals in battery farms. Battery-produced eggs and meat are on the whole and in the short run (in spite of some concealed costs) somewhat cheaper in the West than free-range equivalents. (The difference in egg prices at the time of writing is about 12 per cent.) Competition does therefore exist to the extent of a noticeable, though silent, economic clash, but certainly not to the extent of a life-and-death one. We do, then, have immediately, in this and other cases, problems about the exchange-rate at the species-barrier. I shall discuss this later, suggesting that this rate can indeed not be set quite at par – that 'speciesism' is not just an irrational prejudice – but that that is no reason for letting it zoom to the other extreme and justify absolute dismissal.

It seems important, too, to set cases like these against their real economic background, which has changed radically since our current typecast ideas about such things as meat-eating were formed. Vegetarians, although their numbers have greatly increased, are still often thought of, somewhat tribally, as a set of eccentrics who prefer animal interests to human ones. But the most striking reasons for not eating meat are now those concerned with human welfare. It is enormously extravagant to use grains, beans, pulses and so forth for animal food, and then eat the animals, rather than letting human beings eat the grains etc. right away. In the present food shortage, and still more in the sharper ones which threaten us, human interests demand most strongly that this kind of waste should be stopped.[7]

The difficulty in doing anything about this rests largely on the inertia of custom, and particularly on the tribal way of thinking which I just mentioned. This really needs attention. On the face of things, it may look as if vegetarians might do better to be less concerned with commitment to absolute abstention, and more with steady, positive propaganda in favour of eating more vegetables and less meat – a policy to which many other sorts of consideration already converge strongly. To some extent this is already happening, as a result of rising costs, of health considerations and of a less hidebound style of cookery. And since effective changes of custom are always gradual, it might seem best just to encourage the trend. There is, however, a further very interesting difficulty. The symbolism of meat-eating is never neutral. To himself, the meat-eater seems to be eating life. To the vegetarian, he seems to be eating death. There is a kind of gestalt-shift between the two positions which makes it hard to change, and hard to raise questions on the matter at all without becoming embattled. I think that the only way to deal with this kind of symbolism is to recognize it, and to try to separate its irrational from its rational elements. Things are made harder still by an extra, very widespread element of social symbolism. Meat-eating indicates success and prosperity, therefore hospitality. Medical opinion, too, used to proclaim the need for plenty of meat and dairy-products, though it has now for some time been shifting towards proclaiming chiefly their dangers. The number of hale and thriving vegetarians around should always have made it plain that you do not die without meat, but there is still a widespread conviction that you probably do. The original symbolism, depicting a straight life-and-death clash between animals and man, is still very strong. It undoubtedly forms one of the main difficulties for many people in taking the animal issue seriously at all. Thus, although both for people and animals a steady movement towards eating *less* meat is needed, and although what the animals need most urgently is probably a campaign for treating them better before they are eaten, a tribal division into total eaters and total abstainers still tends strongly to capture our imagination.

Rather similar trouble arises about opposition to animal experiments. Here a most savage dispute arose in the last century. Much of its fury seems to have been due to the strangely anti-rational stance taken by

Claude Bernard, the great French physiologist, who flatly refused to defend by argument his systematic total disregard of distress and pain in his unanaesthetized animals, proclaiming simply that it was the attitude proper for scientists, who should therefore refuse to discuss the matter at all with anybody except their like-minded colleagues.[8] (The first anti-vivisection society in Europe seems to have been founded by Bernard's own wife and daughters, who had come home to find that he had vivisected the domestic dog.) Bernard's purely tribal approach to a topic which is after all not beyond the scope of reason has fortunately been gradually giving way to more intelligent and open-minded methods, under the influence of a changing attitude to animals. Both sides now acknowledge the need to meet each other's arguments. It must emerge that some experiments are much more justifiable than others.[9] The feat of justification cannot, in any case, be performed merely by raising an umbrella marked 'Science'. It demands attention to the actual benefits which can reasonably be expected, and a serious comparison of the conflicting values involved.

5   THE COMPLEXITY OF MORAL CLAIMS

About the lifeboat model, a word more should probably still be said. It is important to see that I am not at all denying the seriousness of the problem. The difficulty of redressing gross human inequalities is real, vast and terrible; it may well prove too much for us altogether. In the face of this fact, which has loomed up somewhat suddenly on us after a century or two of optimism, lifeboat thinking expresses a very natural reaction of simple despair. It suggests that we simply write off all the outer reaches of concern, employing an apparently very simple diagram (Figure 1). Simplicity is always attractive, but here, as I have suggested, it is misleading. Who constitutes *us*? How wide is the inner circle? If we concentrate simply on possible competition, we shall find that this can arise at any point, and to be safe against it we shall have to arrive at an even simpler diagram (Figure 2). Now this heroic terminus of competitive thinking is indeed a possible starting-point for political theory, as Hobbes showed. It is the basis of social-contract thought, and we shall be discussing its strengths and weaknesses later. But it is no help at all when we consider the larger groupings which we might find it worth our while to make, and the units with which we might consent to identify. To work on this problem, other principles will be needed, and we cannot avoid making things more complex. We might try, for instance, a series of concentric circles (Figure 3). But at once we see that the order of the circles is not at all certain. At each point we may want to reverse it, or be dissatisfied with either order. Further groupings constantly occur to us, and, at every stage, it seems that some groupings are more important

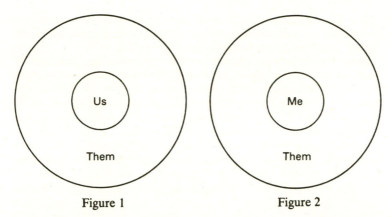

Figure 1   Figure 2

for some purposes, some for others. The concentric arrangement will not work at all. We must imagine instead a set of overlapping figures of varying shapes, representing various *kinds* of claims and loyalties. At

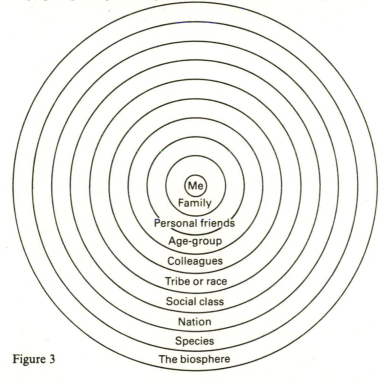

Figure 3

this point diagrams become much harder, and I shall use only a deliberately simplified one, showing a few of the kinds of claim which happen to concern our problem (Figure 4).

There is obviously no simple formula for determining priority among these distinct kinds of claim, and moral philosophies like Utilitarianism which try to make the job look simple can only deceive us. Each culture, and each individual, must and does work out a map, a quite complex set of principles for relating them. Overlaps certainly tend to make claims stronger. But they do not necessarily fix priorities, because relatively isolated claims must sometimes prevail, when they are very strong, over weaker ones which come nearer to the centre of the web because they have been institutionalized. This happens particularly often in the case of 'special need'. By this term I mean any grave misfortune, such as that

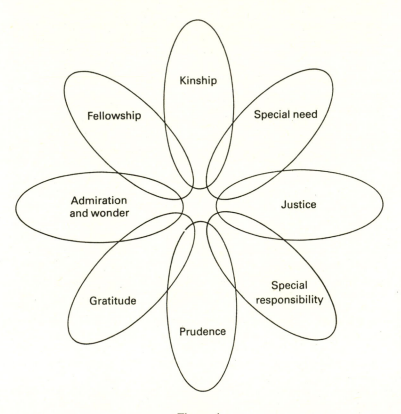

Figure 4

which the Samaritan recognized in the injured traveller's case. On a political scale, this is the sort of claim which, as Robert McNamara has suggested, arises from the 'absolute poverty' of many people in the Third World – that is, not from just any sort of inequality, but from real hopeless destitution.[10] By 'special responsibility', I mean claims arising from our own acts and the acts of those with whom we identify. These are claims of the kind which rest on someone who has, for instance, taken charge of somebody else's life to the extent of persuading him to change his dwelling-place or his occupation. Politically, this sort of claim affects, for instance, a colonial power which has for its own advantage altered its subjects' life-style irreversibly, or even a large-scale buyer which has done the same thing. Both these sorts of claim can arise without blood-relation, acquaintance or admiration, and can on occasion be strong enough to override all these considerations. (Thus, the Samaritan's efforts may make him late for supper at his venerable uncle's, or even make him spend the money which was meant for his uncle's present, without thereby becoming unjustified or mistaken.)

What, then, about animals? Both these sorts of claim can, it seems, arise in their case too. They can be in terrible need, and they can be brought into that need by human action. When they are, it is not obvious why the absence of close kinship, acquaintance or the admiration which is due to human rationality should entirely cancel the claim. Nor do we behave as if they obviously did so. Someone who sees an injured dog lying writhing in the road after being hit by a car may well think, not just that he will do something about it, but that he ought to. If he has hit it himself, the grounds for this will seem still stronger. It is not obvious that his reasons for thinking like this are of a different kind from those that would arise if (like the Samaritan) he saw an injured human being. And he too may feel about equally justified in both cases in being late for his uncle's party. It would be rather an odd response to such a situation for someone (who was not actually rushing off on a life-or-death mission) to drive past, ignoring the human or animal casualty, on the grounds that his resources of compassion are limited, and there may be more deserving cases somewhere else. The reason why this would be odd is that compassion does not need to be treated hydraulically in this way, as a rare and irreplaceable fluid, usable only for exceptionally impressive cases. It is a habit or power of the mind, which grows and develops with use. Such powers (as is obvious in cases like intelligence) are magic fluids which increase with pouring. Effective users do not economize on them. Among the humanitarian reformers who have spoken out most strongly for animals there are many, such as Voltaire, Wilberforce, Shaftesbury, Bentham, Mill, Bernard Shaw, who have also been front-rank campaigners for the rights of human beings.

Such people have always resisted the despair which gives rise to lifeboat thinking; this is how they have achieved things which, in their times, appeared entirely impossible.

The model of concentric circles dividing *us* from *them* remains, however, very influential. One of its most popular forms is the idea that concern for *them* beyond a certain limit – and in particular concern for animals – is not serious because it is purely a matter of emotion. The view of emotion implied by this sort of thinking is an odd one. We will look at this suggestion in the next chapter.

3 Emotion, Emotiveness and Sentimentality

I THE STIGMA OF EMOTION

What does it mean to say that scruples on behalf of animals are merely emotional, emotive or sentimental? What else ought they to be?

Charges of this kind are a very common way of dismissing these scruples, and other scruples as well. Just what these charges mean, however, is not so clear as one might suppose. We badly need to get it clear, because the relation between emotion and reason is a very central crux of our lives. What else, besides emotion, is in general needed for a valid scruple, and how is its presence detected? 'Emotivist' theories of ethics have suggested that morality altogether is nothing but the expression of emotion, or of attitudes formed from it.[1] If this were right, the complaint that scruples about animals were only this would be vacuous. But is it vacuous? What does it mean? We had better consider some examples. Here, for a start, is a piece from an article about controversy over the conditions of battery chickens (italics are mine throughout):

A. The ammunition consists largely of several rounds of *emotion* followed by a quick burst of *uninformed* allegations about costs . . . For some people, the subject will always be an *emotive* one. Birds which cannot spread their wings or indulge their instincts to scratch arouse public indignation and sympathy. Yet . . . many consumers have been quite ready to accept the benefits of factory farms.[2]

Next, with slightly more attempt at subtlety, part of a scientist's defence against criticisms of his piece of research entitled 'Development of Grooming in Mice with Amputated Forelimbs':

B. X's letter appears to treat the *dual issues of rationality and sensitivity* in our dealings with nature, and as such is an *important emotional expression*. However, I am surprised at his unawareness of the importance [of the work; a defence of which follows] . . . Because of my concern for the animals' welfare, I rejected possible alternatives, including technically difficult and potentially devastating central lesions (which would have been hidden and thus might have caused less *emotional reaction* on the part of observers). The

33

fact that the animals in this study, by all available criteria, lived a full and apparently well-adjusted life . . . suggests that *surface emotional reactions* may not be sufficient for either a rational or humane orientation to the world in which we live.[3]

Next comes a piece which is rather different, because the scruples involved are ecological rather than humane and might just as well have applied to plants:

C. The trouble with wildlife conservation today is the same as when it first gained impetus as a movement in the late 50s, namely that it draws *emotive opinions* into what should be *objective discussions* . . . Conservationists ought to touch down occasionally from their flights of *euphoric fancy* to realize that the nation must plan its land-use to best effect (including ecological assessments) and that it *cannot afford* the *luxury* of ill-used or inappropriately used acreage on any large scale. In opposing the prospect of forested uplands in Scotland, Y neglects the fact that those uplands were once forested by nature and have since been *miserably* denuded by man (and beast). Is there any landscape more *desolate and bleak* than that of the southern uplands of Scotland?[4]

Then, because it is important to understand the charge in quite general terms, I add a piece (self-explanatory I think) on a quite different topic:

D. . . . material was presented in a *needlessly biassed and sensational form.* All these things tend to reduce morale and the quality of intelligence work . . . I feel frankly that, in 1979, it is high time that the name of the Agency was changed. CIA, those three initials have become what we in the US refer to as a *buzz word.* It isn't a word, but they're buzz initials. You say 'CIA' and that immediately *triggers images* of the Bay of Pigs, and the demise of Allende in Chile . . . Why do we have to harness CIA operations? Because we don't trust our President, because we don't trust our Director? Because power corrupts? *These things sound so nice* when they're said in the old halls of academia . . .

    Americans want a strong intelligence organization; they feel their Government should know what's going on in the world. On the other hand, they don't much like hearing about dirty tricks or the connivery that is involved in espionage. *They'd be delighted to have the operation run and not hear too much about it.*[5]

What charges are actually being made here? We all feel that some accusation or other is present. This impression is so strong that people often find that their most natural response is denial. We incline to say at once, 'I have absolutely no emotion in the matter,' and to say this even when it is plainly false. ('Damn you, I haven't lost my temper.') We do that, of course, in order to avoid the related but much stronger charge of being actually overcome and carried away by emotion, of being so emotional that our thought is paralysed.

Now the word *emotion* and still more *emotional* certainly can be used for such violent and incapacitating states ('Don't get emotional'). But these words are just as often, or even more often, used in a wide and more neutral sense for all sorts of feeling, strong and weak. The word *sentiment* has the same ambiguity. Our emotional life includes the whole range of our feelings, motives and sympathies. This whole range, obviously, is not something which paralyses thought or any of our other faculties. It is the power-house which keeps the whole lot going. In this wide sense there is nothing objectionable about emotion at all; quite the contrary. Accordingly, anyone accused of being emotional about injustice or oppression or war or bad science or anything else can quite properly reply, 'Of course I feel strongly about this, and with good reason. It is a serious matter. Anyone who has no feeling about it, who does not mind about it, has got something wrong with him.' Strong feeling is fully appropriate to well-grounded belief on important subjects. Its absence would be a fault. This is the element of truth in Emotivism; morality does require feeling. The Emotivist's mistake is in supposing that it requires nothing else; in trying to detach such feelings from the thoughts that properly belong to them.[6]

2   MORE THOUGHT NOT LESS FEELING

It might be better if we made this move of admitting appropriate feeling more often. As it is, the idea does sometimes get around that merely having strong feelings is, in itself, a fault in controversy. The real fault must lie, not in the presence of feeling, but in the absence of thought, or in the unsuitability of feeling to thought. The word *emotion* is slightly troublesome here, because we do not tend to use it much of ourselves. The verb, as commonly conjugated, seems to run: 'I am convinced – you are excited – he is getting emotional.' Our own feeling, particularly when we are sure it *is* suitable, does not seem to call for comment. But what matters for controversial purposes, as we all know when we think about it, is not its strength but its suitability.

Things are very similar if we turn from the question of *being emotional* (or sentimental) to that of *being emotive*. Here the charge shifts from that of wallowing in emotion oneself to that of trying to produce it in other people. Now this attempt in itself is not wrong. All argument involves trying to change feelings, because all belief involves feeling. Even a scientist or historian, if he thinks a colleague is making a mistake, can quite properly try to *rouse his suspicions* on the matter, to *make him unhappy* about the error, to *weaken his confidence* in it, to *rouse his curiosity* about an alternative suggestion and eventually to induce a *confident acceptance* of it. In itself, this is quite a proper aim.

In fact, it is a service which we all owe each other in cases where we are genuinely convinced that there is a mistake. The wrongness lies in attempting such enterprises for the wrong reasons and by the wrong methods – in trying to produce the emotion itself directly, by non-rational methods, rather than to argue honestly and openly about the issues. The word *emotive* is actually itself something of a buzz-word, coined specially to label these wrong cases. What stinks, then, is not actually the attempt to alter feeling, but the absence of the only sort of context which can justify this. That context requires genuine beliefs to which those feelings would be appropriate, and willingness to argue these beliefs on their own merits.

There is however another misleading idea which distorts both the charge of emotion and that of emotiveness, namely, an impression that strong feeling is in itself more objectionable than calm feeling, and that states of indifference, involving no feeling, would really be the best of all. In which state is it better that serious political debating should go on? Here again, what really matters is surely not (apart from extremes) the strength of the emotion, but its suitability. Anyone who reports a danger to people who have not yet noticed it is liable to be called emotional or emotive. If sincere, he is himself frightened, and he is quite properly trying to produce fright in others. Fright is the emotion appropriate to his beliefs; he has reason for it. Does that make him unreliable? The case is common:

> E'en such a man, so pale, so woebegone,
> Drew Priam's curtain in the dead of night
> And would have told him, half his Troy was burned –

He was emotional all right, and also apparently emotive. Was that a fault? Suppose that at this point someone else appears and reassuringly explains that it is all an idle rumour, what are we to say about him? Actually, he is a spy in the pay of the enemy, plotting to keep Priam quiet in bed till the Greeks have control of the city . . . He is not a bit emotional (why should he be? His side is winning). And towards Priam, his aims do not seem emotive. He is trying after all to produce calm, to get rid of emotion. But of course he still embodies all the objectionable part of emotiveness. He is trying to work directly on emotion for his own ends, by-passing normal thought. (Compare sub-liminal suggestion.) Again, what is really wrong is the attack on thought, and it would be much better to say so. This fellow is a traitor and a fraud. These perfectly adequate descriptions of what is wrong with him do not need any mention of emotiveness to complete them.

In general, then, the charge we are analysing seems to be one of introducing *inappropriate* feelings into controversy. Clearly, this does not only happen in cases involving animals. Is there any reason to suppose that it must always happen there, that all emotion is inappropriate to animals, and that, if it occurs, it is false, and is merely being indulged in for its own sake? (That indulgence would be sentimentality.) This strange view is a form of absolute dismissal. If it is to be argued, it will have to wait for Chapter 4. More modestly, the point may be that the particular feeling expressed at the time is inappropriate to the particular case. This often is what is meant, and in detail this charge often turns out to concern only two quite limited reasons for inappropriateness – ignorance and insincerity. In themselves, these charges are serious. Both of them, however, need suitable evidence. And both are much better made under their own names, without the red herring of reference to emotion.

3 EMOTION AND IGNORANCE

Let us now look at the extracts which I gave at the start of this chapter, to see typical examples of these two charges. The charge of ignorance is particularly prominent in example B. To answer his critics, the author puts forward three propositions of which he considers they have shown their ignorance. These are:

1. that his research is very important,

2. that he could have done it by methods still more objectionable, and

3. that the method which he did use did not damage the mice as much as those other methods would have done – indeed, 'by all available criteria', it did not damage them at all.

Had the critics known these truths (he implies) they would not have made fools of themselves by getting so excited. In calling their response an 'important emotional expression', he seems to mean that it would have been appropriate but for the above-named facts, and that this might actually have consequences for other, less admirable, research. So he is not an absolute dismisser.

It is worth looking briefly at his arguments, because they illustrate the grotesque standard of reasoning commonly found in such defences, something from which accusations about emotion often distract attention. Argument 1 is of course relevant, but is unfortunately not much use, since all researchers suppose their own work to be important, and (as those responsible for allotting grants etc. well know) nearly all of them can make a case for it which sounds at least as plausible as this one to people outside the field. To cut any ice, the pleas need to be supported by good explanations of how this crucial topic has to be explored *by these particular methods*. This involves showing a field of inquiry so structured as to have reached a bottle-neck. No attempt is made to do this. Instead, the author's vague remarks about possible alternative methods culminate in argument 2 – that there were still nastier methods which he could have used. This presumably is always true. It can therefore scarcely do him much good, especially as he rashly lets out that they were more difficult anyway. The main point of this suggestion seems to be its bearing on point 3, which is the nub of his case. Here he accuses his critics of ignorance about what does and what does not actually constitute damage to mice. It is noteworthy that he rightly treats this, not as a matter of taste, but as a factual question on which it is possible to be mistaken. Some imaginary observers might, he says, make a mistake about it, supposing his method to be nastier than a particular alternative one, merely because its effects are more obvious. Since his attackers are not actually these observers at all, but are scientists who have read his reports, this is a complete red herring. It serves, however, to evoke a picture of ignorant, superficial criticism ('surface emotional reactions') – of rustics gaping in at the dentist's window and supposing that he is assaulting his patient. The real truth (he continues), which those rustics failed to see, is that 'by all available criteria, the mice lived a full and apparently well-adjusted life'. All criteria (that is) except having forelegs . . .? This recalls a remark which used often to be made about the early films of thalidomide children. How well they manage (the commentators used to marvel), how lively they are, how active and sociable they contrive to be! Nobody, however, has ever thought that this could be made into a defence of thalidomide, or could show that deprivation of limbs did not matter.

The issue here is about what constitutes damage and welfare for a given species. It is one which can be quite important in animal cases, and it is of course true in general that people can make mistakes about it, and can suppose an animal to be ill-treated when it is not. For instance, someone who heard that a particular zoo's python had not eaten for a year might well suppose that it was being starved, or at least that its appetite was affected by illness. But he would be wrong; pythons are like that. Similarly, it might seem cruel to keep a mother rabbit apart from her babies except for one visit a day. But it would not be; she only visits them once a day in any case. And so on. Such questions (as I have pointed out) are factual ones, not matters of taste or ones calling for an existential decision. (Talk of 'fact–value distinctions' is not very helpful here.) Of course there are always border-line cases. But in general, the way to find out what is good or bad for a given species, what constitutes a normal, healthy life for it, is intelligent, informed observation. It must, however, be the full, systematic observation of a zoologist prepared to be interested in the species for its own sake, not casually for purposes of exploitation. And in these days, it ought to take advantage of the disciplined skills of ethology.[7] If somebody equipped, with these skills were to come forward with such an extraordinary proposition as that mice did not really need their forelegs, he would have to bring much better evidence than the adapted behaviour of amputees. It is well known that young creatures have an amazing power of adapting to early mutilations, and that this could not prove the process to be no injury. But of course the commoner situation is that where a scientist working in another field, who merely uses the creatures and does not study them, casually throws out this sort of suggestion. He has then no more right to be listened to than he would have if he made similar suggestions about people. It is he, not his critics, who shows ignorance.

Things are rather similar with the battery hens in the first extract. The authors do not so explicitly accuse those who object to battery conditions of being ignorant about hens, but what they say scarcely makes sense unless they do want to bring that accusation. One does not say that '*for some people* the subject will always be an emotive one' when one means that these people are those properly informed about the subject. This wording strongly suggests that the people in question are ones who just happen to have a peculiar background or emotional constitution. Again, to speak next of '*public* indignation and sympathy' suggests still more strongly that these excitable creatures are not experts, but ignorant citizens. It seems to follow that 'birds which cannot spread their wings and indulge their instincts to scratch' would arouse the misguided sympathy only of these proles, while the real experts would know better. This is the direct opposite of the truth. People unused to birds might think that all was well, because they could not distinguish deprived birds from normal ones, and do not know what is *not* going on that ought to be. Those who do understand birds know the importance of these activities so well, and have made it so clear, that it is against English law to keep any bird in conditions where it cannot perform them – except poultry, which are exempted purely for commercial reasons, not for scientific ones.

4   EMOTION AND INSINCERITY

The main charge brought in this extract (and also in D) is however that of insincerity. We must look at it next. Here the objector does not deny that the feeling expressed by those with scruples is appropriate, nor that their information is correct. He just denies that the feeling itself is strong or persistent enough to deserve attention. 'These scruples,' he says, 'are mere hot air. You are profiting by this institution, and will no doubt continue to do so. Your collusion disqualifies you from criticizing it.'

This point has, of course, nothing specially to do with animals. It is one that can be made on any moral question, but it is always a point about the disputers, not about the dispute. The objector simply makes a prediction about his opponents' scruple – namely, that it will continue to be outweighed by their avarice, laziness or greed. He does not ask whether it ought to be. He just asks them, how much do they really mind? The question is a proper and important one. But it is quite mad to suppose – as people seem to – that some sort of trap prevents the answer 'yes, I do mind a lot, and now let's do something about it'. People who want change are not disqualified from asking for it by their involvement in existing institutions. If they were, no change could ever be brought about. Thus, when Lord Shaftesbury began his agitation for the Factory Acts, it would have been no use for the mill-owners to resist reform by saying to the reformers, 'You are wearing clothes which we have made and will probably go on buying more, so you have no right to complain of our methods.'

When a product – whether clothes, eggs, meat, medicine or the CIA – is produced by iniquitous means, the people who consume that product are among the first who do have a right to complain about it. They are being made jointly responsible. It is their business to demand that the producer should find less objectionable ways of producing it. His business is to try to do this. Only if he has shown, carefully and convincingly, that there are no such ways, and found that his clients still insist on the product, can he shift any share of his own discredit onto them. Certainly they must in the end accept their share of the costs involved. But so must he, and the first move is with him. He cannot block criticism merely by swearing that his methods are the only possible ones, and that any reform must be at the consumers' expense. Experience has shown that people with vested interests can never be trusted on such questions. The mill-owners did not actually founder in their predicted general bankruptcy after the Factory Acts, nor did prices rise disastrously. Welfare veal, humanely produced, turns out to cost less than veal from calves crammed into crates and unable to lie down.[8] Nobody loses except the crate manufacturers and their existing customers, and they not much. It is just that nobody thought of trying it before.

To sum up this point about sincerity in general, it is quite true that 'he who wills the end wills the means also',[9] but this never stops us willing a change of means. Those with a vested interest in the means, however, naturally tend to claim that this change is impossible, and to suggest that this fact is so well known that people demanding it cannot mean what they say. Extract D illustrates this process with an almost lyric elegance; it seems a shame to spoil the effect by comment, but a few remarks are called for. Heims's argument rests entirely on dealing with feeling instead of thought, on ignoring all conceptual links between his opponents' disgust and the undisputed facts to which it is an appropriate response. He treats the disgust merely as an unlucky natural phenomenon, caused by the 'triggering of images' (as it might be by a bad smell), and proposes a piece of psychological engineering to remove the trigger. This move is meant to isolate the feeling from its grounds. He then proclaims its isolation from all practical bearing, from any genuine will for change, thereby dismissing it, not just as a feeling, but as a trivial feeling, not meant to affect action. (This is a charge of sentimentality.) Against such feelings, arguments are out of place, so he does not argue. He simply claims that his countrymen are already as convinced as he is that his methods are the only possible ones. They are, therefore, already his collaborators, kept from admitting their convictions only by hypocrisy. The accusation of hypocrisy is often quite an effective way of silencing critics and making them feel ashamed. We should resist it. During any reform, when people are beginning to notice that something is wrong and trying to see how to alter it, some confusion and inconsistency between theory and practice is normal. It is even necessary. This is not yet hypocrisy. The kind of hypocrisy which invalidates criticism is a deliberate, chronic condition, that of somebody who has settled finally back into accepting the *status quo*. The normal confused condition is uncomfortable but transient. We can always alter practice rather than theory.

5   THE ISSUE OF INAPPROPRIATENESS

In giving rather short shrift to these particular writers' charges of ignorance and insincerity, I am not, of course, suggesting that reformers do not need to be well informed and honest. They do. I am just pointing out that these special limited charges – which require their own evidence – never follow from the general accusation, if it is an accusation, of being emotional. I have suggested that the real charge, which that accusation expresses rather badly, is one of introducing *inappropriate* feeling into controversy.

Now there certainly are real questions, arising all over the moral field, about what feeling actually is appropriate. How much ought we to mind about the preservation of wilderness? or about art? or about the beauty of the countryside? How important is knowledge, or freedom? Ought they always to give way to the contentment of the greater number? How, in general, are conflicts between such various values to be resolved? These are real and serious moral questions.

Accordingly, people who try to deal with them (like the author of extract C) merely in terms of the presence or absence of emotion as such, fall instructively flat on their faces. He objects to 'emotive opinions' and demands an 'objective discussion'. He then defends his own eccentric preference for spruce monoculture by the use of emotive words like 'miserably . . . desolate and bleak' and insinuates, falsely, that it will constitute a return to primitive conditions. Examined more closely, he is seen to be a lifeboat man (see Chapter 2). He operates with a simple contrast between values which he sees as unreal ('euphoric fancy') and real ones – namely, those of economics, what we can afford. This notion of reality as co-extensive with economics is the one that brought Howard Hughes to his wretched solitary death, and which indeed more generally has given us the word 'miser' – literally, a miserable person. Money is a useful means, but it cannot possibly be an end, let alone the only real end of life. It is not actually particularly real; you certainly can't eat it. A romantic obsession with it does indeed give meaning to some people's lives. But there is no sort of reason for the rest of us to accept their short cut through the business of understanding and comparing values.

6   THE PLACE OF FEELING IN MORALITY

These questions about priority among values are the central business of morality. They are not our business here and now, because we are still concerned, in this chapter, with getting animals an admission ticket to the moral scene at all. We are still confronting the rationalist notion that they fall outside it. On this view (which we shall discuss directly in the next chapter) morality is entirely a contract between rational beings. Feeling has no part in it and cannot concern it. And animals concern us only through feeling.

This is a most odd and lop-sided view of morality. There are all kinds of things wrong with it, of which trouble over animals is only a small part, though a very illuminating one. As often happens over lop-sided notions, it has been answered by another, equally unbalanced towards the other side. This is Emotivism, which makes morality entirely a matter of feeling.

Nothing forces us to accept either of these over-simplifications. We have to do justice to both feeling and thought. This means considering them together, and as aspects of the same process. For instance, the thought that a great danger threatens has not been completed – is not yet a proper thought – unless it includes some fear and some wish for action. And fear which includes no thought at all about the nature of the danger is incomplete fear. It is more of a physical state than a proper feeling. Similarly, real indignation is not just an emotional state, but one formed by and containing the thought of the special sort of outrage which calls for it. No separate nuts and bolts are needed to screw these two elements together.

Rationalists however, when they speak of feelings, seem to concentrate only on those emotional states whose completing thought is much less clear. These states are the target for the kind of argument we have been considering. And of course they do occur. The kind of indefinite fear just mentioned exists, though it is not common. And feelings like disgust at blood and wounds can be mere physical reactions. We can feel them at surgical procedures we entirely approve of. And it is often hard – especially for people like us who are seldom confronted with bloodshed – to be sure whether this kind of feeling has any meaning or not. If it never had, it seems that we ought always to ignore it and try to get over it. At least we would never be justified in objecting to the actions which caused it. (Thus people with a physical revulsion to cats do not think that their feeling shows that cats are wicked, or even that cat-keeping is so. It is just that they are sometimes a nuisance, like noise.) But it seems clear that, in fact, disgust at bloodshed often does have a meaning. It has played a great part in the development of more humane behaviour, because it can alert people's imagination to what they are doing, and wake their sympathies for the victims. The same thing happens with unthinking revulsions to unfairness, meanness, ingratitude, envy and the like. The revulsion itself is not significant, but it can become so in the context of fuller thought. Real scruples, and eventually moral principles, are developed out of this kind of raw material. They would not exist without it. This is the answer to our question at the outset about what *more*, besides feeling, a valid scruple requires.

It will not do, therefore, to keep the two things separate – to write, as extract B does, about 'the dual issues of rationality and sensitivity' if this means that they can be handled apart. Sensitivity requires rationality to complete it, and vice versa. There is no siding onto which emotions can be shunted so as not to impinge on thought.

People sometimes try to provide such a siding by treating questions which they find it hard to think about as aesthetic. Extract C suggests this view of ecological scruples. Certainly aesthetic considerations can often be separated from moral ones; trains of reasoning may well sit on such a siding. But these trains are only waiting to come back onto the main moral line and approach the question: how much do aesthetic considerations matter when weighed against others? Questions about animals, if similarly parked on a siding marked 'Emotion', will do the same. Feeling is not going to take us out of the moral universe. It is not possible to keep two parallel independent systems of values – one aesthetic or emotional and the other rational or moral

– and prevent their ever meeting. We cannot do this because each of us has only one life to live. We must therefore sometimes settle priority questions *between* emotional or aesthetic values and values of other kinds. To compare and relate these various kinds is the central business of morality, which is itself the weigher, not an item on one of the scales.

4 The Rationalist Tradition (1): Absolute Dismissal

I HARD-LINE DISMISSAL

To find a full, clear statement of the case for excluding concern for animals from morality, we naturally turn to the great seventeenth-century rationalists, particularly to Descartes and Spinoza. There is no doubt about their views. But the chronic difficulty of the topic confronts us. The most drastic and convinced excluders are also those least interested in arguing for their position. They find it obvious. On the other side, Montaigne had argued at length,[1] strongly and quite carefully, against ill-treatment of animals. Descartes, though he probably had Montaigne's remarks in mind, dismissed the subject briskly, as one about which no sensible person would hesitate. Spinoza, with his much greater interest in ethics, did, as we have seen, say rather more. We know, too, that he lived up to his principles, for an early biographer tells us that, being interested in insects, he used often to 'find some spiders and let them fight with one another: or he would find some flies, throw them into the spider's web and watch this battle with great pleasure, even with laughter'. In a letter, he makes a remark about this which should give food for thought about wild-life films:

> Everyone observes with admiration and delight in animals the very things which he detests and regards with aversion in men. For example, the wars of bees, the jealousy of doves, etc., things which we detest in men and for which we nevertheless consider animals more perfect.[2]

As far as it goes, this fits well with the brief argument quoted on p. 10. That argument, however, stands alone in his works, without further explanation, and it raises more problems than it solves. What are these conflicting equal or unequal 'rights' of different species, and how do we know whether they are equal? Just *what* differences in emotions serve to put a creature outside the area of concern? Do they never occur within the human race? What is *reason*? Is it really a single faculty in man, unshared by any animal? And is that faculty really all that we value in humanity? Again, if we met non-human rational creatures, with non-human emotions, how ought we to treat them? What, in any

45

case, is wrong with pity? This last, however, is one of many questions which must find their answers in Spinoza's own rationalistic and egoistic view of morality. He thinks pity in general an evil, first, because it is a feeling, and right actions ought to be produced by thought, second, because pity is painful, and it is the business of each to seek his own pleasure as a mark of his own good.[3] The idea that sympathy might be a natural and proper link between suffering and rejoicing fellow-creatures is alien to his atomizing ethic. Like Descartes' notions about consciousness and personal identity, Spinoza's view of sympathy, and of feeling in general, is needed to explain his dismissal of animals. For anyone who does not share his general position, however, it may seem bizarre and incompatible with a reasonable view of our relations with people. Spinozan rationalists must buy it, but the rest of us may well not want to.

2   COMPLICATING FACTORS

Even rationalism, too, does not speak with a single voice. Leibniz dissents. It was his main philosophic business to object to the yawning gulf which both Descartes and Spinoza had placed between mind and matter, and to object to it on rational grounds, because it made life as a whole unintelligible. He stressed the continuity between intellect and other forms of consciousness, and between non-conscious and conscious life. His reason for mentioning animals, therefore, was usually to show them as life-forms differing from people only in degree. And he, too, seems to have lived up to his principles. 'Herr von Leibniz never killed a fly, however much it inconvenienced him, because he thought it would be a misdeed to destroy so ingenious a mechanism.'[4] And, as Kant reports, 'Leibniz used a tiny worm for purposes of observation, and then carefully replaced it with its leaf on the tree, so that it should not come to harm through any act of his. He would have been sorry – a natural feeling for a humane man – to destroy such a creature for no reason.'[5] These accounts are too brief to show his reasoning, but they show the ambivalence latent in rationalism. On its negative, destructive side it can be extremely savage, writing off at a stroke whatever falls outside the scope of reason. But, on its constructive side, it may find reason at work everywhere. Examination of this range is needed before the knife can properly fall. The same ambivalence is central to science. No doubt entomology has profited by both attitudes. The problem of relating them is not simple. Our first need is to become conscious of it.

3 QUALIFYING MOVES

Even seventeenth-century rationalism, then, does not furnish us with a clear and unanimous licence to poison all the pigeons in the park. And as we move on through the eighteenth century, Enlightenment philosophy, looked at in detail, grows ever more disappointing for absolute dismissers. It is not hard to find passages which, on the surface, seem quite ferocious. There are many arguments to show that animals are not entitled to justice, that they do not have rights, or that we can have no duties or obligations to them. To a casual reader, the philosophers' stand may look grim, clear and, up to the time of Bentham and Schopenhauer, almost unanimous.

The casual reader, however, must look more closely. These arguments are usually verbal rather than moral, and they are hardly ever meant as direct treatments of the animal issue. They are normally outlying parts of discussions about the exact meaning of *rights*, *justice*, *duty* and the rest. They come in briefly, and illustratively, as if the position of animals itself were something already well understood, to clarify some important point about the treatment of humans. More important, the authors – though primarily occupied with what is to go on *inside* their boundaries – commonly remark in passing that much of what falls outside will still, in some sense, be serious moral business. It will matter. Justice, rights, duties or whatever do not cover the whole area of grave human concern. This is a necessary part of such arguments, all the more so because each of these particular terms, when debated philosophically, tends to get a more and more restricted sense. Plenty of other important issues besides the animal one fall outside such senses, and it is essential to keep an eye on the outside of one's boundary. Besides, the narrow area occupied is not always the same one. In common speech, words like rights, justice and the rest have very wide and flexible meanings. Philosophers trying to pin them down more narrowly catch many butterflies, not one. We must know just what a particular writer means by these words in order to grasp what he is excluding animals or other candidates *from*. This is why I have so far avoided using these terms, and have spoken more neutrally of *claims made* or *scruples felt* on behalf of animals. It is also why I have chosen for my title a term not yet much used by moral philosophers (though I think it ought to be) and am inquiring widely 'what can matter?'. We will come back to this topic in Chapter 13.

Accordingly, positions which look like moral ones of absolute dismissal, justifying every possible treatment of animals, often turn out to be merely verbal, rather special definitions of particular moral terms. Some examples are given in the rest of this chapter and in the next.

4 JUSTICE

Hume excludes animals (along with some other rather obscure cases) from justice, from possessing 'any right or property', and from 'society, which presupposes a degree of equality'.[6] Before saying this, however, he observes emphatically that we are 'bound by the laws of humanity to give gentle usage to these creatures'. Moreover, this whole argument is part of his determined attempt to cut the notion of justice down to size, to restrict it within unusually narrow limits. It is, he says, an 'artificial virtue', a set of rules, chiefly concerning property, commonly accepted by consent among equals because of its great convenience, but not valid in situations where it ceases to be generally useful.[7] Hume's main aim is to stress that this kind of rule-system is only a means, and therefore a secondary part of morality. Morality exists to produce utility – that is, well-distributed happiness. And the reason for respecting morality at all is not rational necessity – which might be invoked as a separate ground of justice – but feeling. (His view is the ancestor of Emotivism.) For Hume, therefore, exclusion from justice is by no means exclusion from morality. The word 'right', too, is for him a relatively slight one, a legal rather than a moral term. To say that animals can have no 'rights' certainly does suggest that no civic laws can properly be passed to protect them. And in Hume's day there were no such laws. But in saying firmly that we are none the less 'bound by the laws of humanity to give gentle usage to these creatures' he obviously extends morality far beyond the civic law, and makes gentle usage (whatever that may involve) an ordinary binding duty.

This is not surprising. Hume's empiricism led him to resist, quite generally, the grander claims of rationalists about the superiority of human reason. Reasoning, for him, was a modest activity of which animals were, in their degree, quite capable.[7] People might be better at it, but this did not put them in a separate moral universe. Morality, moreover, was for him not primarily an affair of reasoning at all, but of the feelings, especially the 'sentiment of humanity', which is a natural, not an artificial virtue.[7] 'Humanity' is here a wide and rather mysterious term covering a great range of sympathetic feeling. Most of the examples Hume gives of it deal with feeling for fellow-humans. And in principle it would be possible for an absolute dismisser to rule that, if it is a feeling of *humanity*, it cannot have a non-human object. But Hume sees no reason to make this arbitrary move. He treats the question of what beings we can sympathize with and feel indignant about as a genuinely empirical one, to be settled by experience. The present passage shows his answer.

He does not seem to have thought it very important. But it is not surprising that Bentham and Mill, who developed his views and who lived in an age of increasing humanitarianism, did think it important. Concern about suffering was, after all, a dominant motive with them for developing Utilitarian morality, and they did not, any more than Hume, see any reason for excluding animal suffering from the scene. And Mill, as much as Hume, thought it wrong to place justice at the centre of morality; indeed, he thought justice on the whole an obscure and unhelpful concept. Altogether, Hume's exclusion of animals from the sphere of justice leaves them well inside the area of serious concern and the Utilitarianism which stems from Hume has been, quite consistently, the main philosophic champion of their interests. It is people concerned about justice, not those concerned about animals, who may have reason to be alarmed by Hume.

John Rawls, too, a philosopher who has written a monumental book on justice, excludes animals from its scope altogether. And at first sight this exclusion looks more alarming than Hume's because Rawls's conception of justice is not narrow but exceptionally wide. In fact, critics have sometimes complained that in his work it shows signs of taking over the whole of morality. It would, of course, be possible deliberately to extend the notion of justice to make it do this – to treat it as the central and in some sense inclusive virtue, the deepest explanatory moral concept. Plato did that in the *Republic*, but at the cost of defining justice in a very odd way. Rawls, however, explicitly rejects this policy. Towards the end of his book, having developed his very subtle but still essentially contractual theory, he briefly, but not casually, discusses the important things which lie outside it. The passage is so important that I shall simply quote it in full:

> Last of all, we should recall here the limits of a theory of justice. Not only are many aspects of morality left aside, but no account is given of right conduct in regard to animals and the rest of nature. A conception of justice is but one part of a moral view. While I have not maintained that the capacity for a sense of justice is necessary in order to be owed the duties of justice, it does seem that *we are not required to give strict justice* anyway to creatures lacking this capacity. But it does not follow that there are no requirements at all in regard to them, nor in our relations with the natural order. Certainly it is wrong to be cruel to animals and the destruction of a whole species can be a great evil. The capacity for feelings of pleasure and pain and for the forms of life of which animals are capable clearly impose duties of compassion and humanity in their case. I shall not attempt to explain these considered beliefs. They are outside the scope of the theory of justice, and it does not seem possible to extend the contract doctrine so as to include them in a natural way. A correct conception of our relations to animals and to nature would seem to depend upon a theory of the natural order and our place in it. One of the tasks of metaphysics is to work out a view of the world which is suited for this purpose; it should identify and systematize the truths decisive for these questions. How far justice as fairness will have to be revised to fit into this larger theory it is impossible to say. But it

seems reasonable to hope that if it is sound as an account of justice among persons, it cannot be too far wrong when these broader relationships are taken into consideration.[8]

Taken out of context, remarks like the one in italics can give an impression of supporting absolute dismissal. This is misleading. Rawls (writing in 1971) was rightly asking for philosophy to concern itself with a vast background which he saw as including, and indeed in some sense dwarfing, not only his subject, but the whole of ethics. These inquiries are not easy, but since that time many people have been trying to make them.[9]

Within ethics, however, how successful is Rawls's demarcation of the virtues? I cannot here discuss the general merits of his and other contract-based theories of justice. Plainly, however, there are problems about the status of duties contrasted with such justice. On the one hand, clearly there *are* other sorts of duty – courage, kindness, generosity, gratitude, mercy, compassion and the rest, not to mention 'internal' duties such as integrity and self-respect. On the other, the whole language of duty itself is so tangled with that of debt and contract that it easily suggests that all duty derives from justice – in which case the other apparent duties would not be real duties at all. The word *duty* means debt – and surely, we think, one can only contract a debt within a given and agreed property system? The word *obligation* means a bond – primarily one formed by promising. The word *ought* is simply the past tense of *owe*. And the word *just* itself can have a quite general sense, apparently covering the whole of goodness – as when we talk of justification, or of 'the just and the unjust'. The upshot is that, if one concentrates one's attention on justice, everything outside it begins to look slight and optional. The boundary of justice becomes that of morality itself. Duties like mercy and compassion then begin to seem like mere matters of taste, aesthetic preferences, luxuries, delightful and desirable no doubt in times of leisure, but not serious.

As a moment's thought will show, this cannot be right. The vice opposite to these virtues is cruelty, which is not only a real, distinct vice but, in most people's opinion, one of the worst of vices. Greed, meanness, envy, cowardice, sloth, ingratitude and the rest are equally distinct. There is a tendency to draw them all into justice by saying that acts of cruelty, greed etc. are always unjust acts as well. If *unjust* here has its wide sense and means simply *vicious*, there is not much in this. If it has its narrow one it is not true; there can be real conflicts between justice and mercy or generosity. The limited sense in which Shylock uses the word 'justice' is a normal and useful one.[10] His critics speak quite properly in reminding him of mercy and compassion, rather than complaining that his notion of justice is too narrow. And, as Rousseau reasonably said, 'gratitude is a duty which ought to be paid, but not a right to be exacted'.[11] There are real difficulties about Rawls's enterprise of studying the one virtue, justice, on its own, without a background discussion of its neighbours and of what, in general, a virtue is. So treated, it is almost bound to expand in a way that obscures the claims of the other virtues.

Rawls is not alone here. This distortion pervades the mainstream of eighteenth-century moral thinking, and persists today. The great achievement of the Enlightenment was to build a theory of the Rights of Man which made possible enormous advances towards social justice. In this theory a certain area of morality – the nature of bargains made by rational consent between articulate, self-interested, contracting parties who are equals in power – monopolizes attention. What lies outside that lit circle gets neglected. This process will become clearer if we consider another term whose use it restricts, namely Duty.

5 DUTY

Here the restricter is Kant, denying that there can really be duties to animals. Writing in 1780, more than a century after Spinoza's death, he takes for granted a very different general attitude to suffering from that forced on Spinoza by the brutality and insecurity of the Wars of Religion. About animals, Kant calls in practice for responsible behaviour, and even for something approaching justice. His difficulty is to find a theory to explain this, since morality for him is essentially a transaction between rational beings, and duty a rational bond. Still, he does his best:

> So far as animals are concerned, we have no direct duties. Animals are not self-conscious, and are there merely as a means to an end. That end is man. We can ask, 'Why do animals exist?' But to ask 'Why does man exist?' is a meaningless question. Thus, if a dog has served his master long and faithfully, his service, on the analogy of human service, deserves reward, and when the dog has grown too old to serve, his master ought to keep him till he dies. Such action helps to support us in our duties towards human beings, where they are bounden duties . . . If a man shoots his dog because the animal is no longer capable of service, *he does not fail in his duty to the dog, for the dog cannot judge*, but his act is inhuman and damages in himself that humanity which it is his duty to show towards mankind . . . He who is cruel to animals becomes hard also in his dealings with men . . . The more we come in contact with animals, and observe their behaviour, the more we love them, for we see how great is their care for their young. It is then difficult for us to be cruel in thought even to a wolf. Leibniz used a tiny worm for purposes of observation, and then carefully replaced it with its leaf on the tree so that it should not come to harm through any act of his. He would have been sorry – a natural feeling for a humane man – to destroy such a creature for no reason.[12]

Is it possible to set up like this a class of near-duties, actions characteristic of humane men, which are not bounden duties, but merely training requirements, reminders to keep in practice? As we have seen (pp. 16–17) it is hard to understand why failing in a non-duty should have any relevance to performance in a duty. Suppose that the shepherd claims, and can prove, that he actually treats people better when he is allowed to work off his ill-temper on his dogs, and to shoot them the moment they cease to earn their keep? (Dogs have in fact probably served the human race very well in this way, and saved a number of lives.) Kant, himself a humane man, does not want to issue this general licence for redirected aggression. He therefore posits a set of shadowy near-duties to discourage it. But such a status can hardly work. The whole point of a duty is that it is bounden or binding. It may be slight; it may often be overridden by other duties, but so far as it goes it must surely bind us. As Hume says, we are 'bound by the laws of humanity to give gentle usage'. If we narrow the notion of *duty* to cover only contracts between articulate equals, we are going to need some other word to express the binding element in our relations, not just to animals, but to the inarticulate and helpless generally – to children, defectives, lunatics and the old, and also to people with whom we cannot communicate. Schopenhauer – who took Kant very seriously – made some comments which seem relevant here:

> Genuine morality is outraged by the proposition that beings devoid of reason (hence animals) are *things* and therefore should be treated merely as *means* that are not at the same time an *end* . . . Thus only for practice are we to have sympathy for animals, and they are, so to speak, the pathological phantom for the purpose of practising sympathy for human beings. In common with the whole of Asia not tainted with Islam (that is, Judaism) I regard such propositions as revolting and abominable.

Again, discussing the undervaluing of feeling which he rightly sees as producing this distortion, he observes:

> Boundless compassion for all living beings is the firmest and surest guarantee of pure moral conduct, and needs no casuistry . . . If we attempt to say, 'This man is virtuous, but knows no compassion' . . . the contradiction is obvious. Tastes differ, but I know of no finer prayer than the one which ends old Indian dramas (just as in former times English plays ended with a prayer for the King). It runs, 'May all living beings remain free from pain.'[13]

5 The Rationalist Tradition (2): Interests, Rights and Language

I   DUTY AND 'DUTY'

Many later philosophers have followed Kant in rejecting the terminology of *duties* to animals. Their reasons for this are connected with
difficulties over *rights*, which we shall discuss in a moment. Rights are
commonly taken to be correlative with duties, and since the notion of
rights has a technical, legal sense, it is harder to use it out of the
context of organized, articulate bargaining. *Duty*, however, is a much
more general, everyday word, and Kant's attempt to give it a technical
sense here can hardly succeed in the face of ordinary usage. In
common speech, to say that we have no duty to animals (or anyone
else) means that it does not matter how we treat them. It absolves us.
It would be awkward and pedantic to say 'this is just a verbal point –
you are still bound to behave as you would if there was a duty'. And
to say 'behave thus, or your character may be corrupted' would not be
convincing.

To show how natural and useful the language of duties is here, I
quote a passage from R. M. Hare, one of those perfectly reputable
moral philosophers who sees no objection today to using it about
animals. He is not campaigning on behalf of animals; indeed, this
passage is as isolated in his work as Spinoza's is in his. He is merely
illustrating the working of the Golden Rule:

> We recognize certain duties towards both men and animals, but certain
> others towards men only. [Self-government, for instance, is not owed to animals,
> because] we can say, 'If I were turned into an animal, I should stop having any
> desire for political liberty' . . . In all cases the principle is the same – am I
> prepared to accept a maxim which would allow this to be done to me, were I
> in the position of this man or animal, and capable of having only the
> experiences, desires etc. of him or it? [There are, however, various reasons why
> people fail to apply this principle.] A number of different things may have gone
> wrong. The bear-baiter does not really imagine what it is like to be a bear. If
> he did, he would think and act differently . . . These people are not paying

53

attention to the relevant similarities between themselves and their victims . . .
The bear-baiter is not thinking of the bear as his brother – or even cousin.[1]

Not only does Hare find it perfectly natural to talk of duties here, and
to explain them in the same way as all other duties, but he finds none
of that surprising difficulty which Spinoza reported in identifying the
more obvious emotions of animals and seeing which are like our own.
Animals do *not* want or need democratic institutions, but they *do* want
and need not to be tormented. Kant already penetrated this imaginary
barrier easily enough when he remarked 'we love them, for we see how
great is their care for their young'. We do. The similarity between the
emotions of our own and those of other comparable species is quite
strong enough to make sympathy, and the identification of motives,
possible where ordinary care is used. In recent years, Behaviourism has
generated scepticism about this, as about many other similar feats
which we perform successfully every day. Moreover, some philosophers
have recently exaggerated the importance of language to such a point
that they make all inter-species communication look impossible. But
since it takes place, they must be wrong. The human imagination is not
– though no doubt it might have been – so weak as to deny us the
materials for judging what in general suits an animal. Because so much
human communication on such matters is non-verbal anyway, the
absence of speech does not prevent this. Indeed it is often a positive
advantage, because speech is often used to conceal or misrepresent
feelings.

2   INTERESTS

The difficulties of rationalistic rigorism here come out clearly in some
recent attempts to answer demands for animal rights by fencing animals
back into their supposed obscurity behind the language barrier. For
instance, R. G. Frey, in a book with the striking title *Interests and
Rights: The Case Against Animals*,[2] argues as follows: Animals cannot
have rights because they cannot have interests. They cannot have
interests because they cannot have desires or emotions. They cannot
have desires or emotions because they cannot have the thoughts
required for them. And they cannot have those thoughts because they
cannot speak.

All this is simply a verbal or conceptual argument about the proper
use of terms. There is no reasoning to show that these conceptual
decisions ought to affect our behaviour, and indeed Frey sometimes
disclaims any intention to draw such conclusions. Yet the book's subtitle
unmistakably advertises a practical argument. Moreover, Frey's polemic
is directed throughout against Peter Singer and other defenders of

animal rights, who say clearly that their case is a substantial moral one, meant to affect conduct, not just a ruling about the proper use of terms.

It is worthwhile to examine Frey's ladder, and to notice how remote it is from any kinds of consideration which could usefully guide practice. The first two rungs are provided by English law. That law does indeed restrict the terms *right* and *interest* to human beings, but it does so for reasons which are limited and entirely practical. For reasons of convenience, property is supposed always to belong to a responsible person, capable of claiming it and dealing with counter-claimants. The law therefore lays down a principle called *mortmain*, intended in the first place to prevent dead persons, and then other non-articulate beings, from becoming the owners of property. And it defines the words *right* and *interest* in accordance with this principle, because it uses them primarily in relation to property. It there applies them only to human beings.*

Now it is not obvious why this special usage should have any bearing at all on our thought and action in other contexts, any more than the numberless other special uses, which the law constantly requires for ordinary words, are expected to do so. A number of philosophers have, however, taken it as a model for the whole political use of the word. 'Interests,' says H. J. McCloskey,

suggest that which is, or ought to be, or which would be of *concern* to the person/being. It is partly for this reason – because the concept of interests has this evaluative–prescriptive overtone – that we decline to speak of the interests of animals, and speak rather of their welfare.[3]

Thus, unless elephants can show in words that they grasp what their interests are, can estimate their importance correctly and know what ought to be done about them, they have no interests, and therefore no rights. This, the author explains, doesn't necessarily mean that we can ill-treat them. But if it doesn't mean that, what does it mean, and what is the point of saying it?

---

* There is, of course, a wider issue involved here, because the law has sometimes to make arrangements for cases where people wish to give property to a different sort of recipient. Thus, as a leading text-book puts it, 'Difficult problems have arisen where the object of a trust is a non-human beneficiary, such as a dog, an incorporated association, or a non-charitable purpose' (Philip H. Pettit, *Equity and the Law of Trusts*, 3rd edn, Butterworths, 1966, pp. 38–43). Such things as the upkeep of graves and the saying of masses, as well as the welfare of animals, fail to qualify as charity, which is defined as relating only to humans. The law, however, allows certain extensions for such cases by viewing them as gifts to the trustees, conditional on certain functions, which are in general useful to humans. In discussing the animal cases, judges do of course travel beyond the question of usage to the principles which determine this indirect benefit, and they tend to take for granted the rationalist views which we are now discussing (Pettit, pp. 180–83). Legal usage reflects these views. But for that very reason it cannot be called upon to defend them. Their defence must be philosophical.

3 LANGUAGE AND REASONING

There is a point, but it is one not relevant to morals. Contemporary English-speaking philosophers attribute great importance to language for a perfectly good reason. 'Linguistic philosophy' is not, as is sometimes supposed, merely a name for attending to words rather than to reality. (That is a vice which lies in wait, not specially for these philosophers, but for scholars in general.) It refers instead to a special view about the role of language in making the world intelligible. We expect order in the universe, and on the whole we are not disappointed. Traditional rationalism explained this by saying that the world simply was orderly, having been made so by God. But how do we know this? Kant replied that we know it because we know our own faculties, which impose this order on the world in the process of observing it. Any disorderly elements simply could not reach us. In this there is certainly much truth. But it has proved rather difficult to decide just what these ordering faculties are. One suggestion about this – essentially that of Wittgenstein – has in this century turned out particularly powerful and attractive, namely, that the work is largely done by language. To speak of a world is already to have mapped it, and to share one's map with fellow-speakers of one's language. And this is enough to make the development of understanding possible.

This is, I am sure, a profound and useful insight, salvaging essential truths from traditional rationalism. But it is not at all easy to work out in detail, particularly at the border-lines where what can be clearly said gives way to what cannot. If one takes Wittgenstein's early, black-or-white position, everything not fully verbal tends to vanish. ('Everything which can be put into words can be put clearly', and 'What we cannot speak about we must pass over in silence'.⁴) He later abandoned this dogmatic simplicity, and emphasized the extreme complexity of border-line questions. But this is just the area we now have to deal with. The position of other species raises immediate problems. If language were really the only source of conceptual order, all animals except man would live in a totally disordered world. They could not be said to vary in intelligence, since they could not have the use of anything that could reasonably be called intelligence at all. As it is, however, they do vary in intelligence, and each species understands certain aspects of the world very well. This fact surely tells along with the other strong considerations which made Wittgenstein subtilize his views. The truth seems to be that – even for humans – a great deal of the order of the world is pre-verbally determined, being the gift of faculties which we share with other animals. (Babies would be a lot worse off were this not so.) Of course the addition of language builds a magnificent superstructure on this foundation. But it does not replace it.

4   UNDERSTANDING WITHOUT WORDS

I think it is clear that linguistic philosophers have often overstated the case for the dependence of intelligence on language in a way which their arguments do not justify and indeed do not require. Thus, for instance, Max Black, having said that man is the only animal to use symbols, goes on to add that he is 'the only animal that can truly *understand* and *misunderstand*'.[5] Similarly Stuart Hampshire writes, 'It would be senseless to attribute to an animal a memory that distinguished the order of events in the past, and it would be senseless to attribute to it an expectation of an order of events in the future. It does not have the concepts of order, or any concepts at all.'[6] Plainly neither Black nor Hampshire is controverting – or is even interested in – the very large literature of careful discussion by zoologists and psychologists about the different kinds of understanding and conceptual grasp which different sorts of animals actually display. This work would not impress them. Their point is one of definition. They are not prepared to count as *concept* or as *understanding* anything which does not involve speech.

This is still plainer in some striking and much-quoted remarks of Wittgenstein's:

One can imagine an animal angry, frightened, unhappy, happy, startled. But hopeful? And why not?

A dog believes his master is at the door. But can he also believe his master will come the day after tomorrow? – And *what* can he not do here? . . .

Can only those hope who can talk? Only those who have mastered a language. That is to say, the phenomena of hope are modes of this complicated form of life. (If a concept refers to a character in human handwriting, it has no application to beings that do not write.)[7]

Now the general reasoning is clear enough here, but the example chosen will not support anything like such extreme conclusions. It is greatly exaggerated. The terms *hope* and *hopeful* are in fact quite regularly used about animals, not just by idiots, but by careful and systematic observers of animal behaviour. They are not used out of sentimental projection, but because they are needed to describe one important sector of the normal range of moods displayed – a sector no less important in other animals than in man. Hope is surely on the same footing as fear.

What Wittgenstein has in mind, and what is true, is that the use of language can immensely extend and enrich the sense of the past and future. This is indeed one of its central jobs, and the resulting difference is among the most vital and valued of human specialities. But that does not deprive animals of expectation altogether, any more than it deprives them of fear or memory. Nor does it even necessarily deprive them of the count of days. There is, for instance, plenty of evidence of the ability of domestic animals to follow a weekly cycle. Thus, Sheila Hocken's guide-dog quickly and spontaneously learned to take her every Friday, without needing to be told the day, to the places where she did her weekend shopping.[8] More remarkably, feral cats which were fed once a week learned to turn up in advance on the day when the feeds were due.[9] This sort of thing is not really surprising if you think of the complexities of life in the wild. Consider migrations, pregnancies, seasons, brief harvests and the constant need to anticipate the movements of prey or predators. Many animals move continually from one food source to another, often with their young to provision, and sometimes with responsibility for a whole pack or herd. They have to be able to think how long this or that will last, or when it will recur. If they had not enough memory and anticipation of order to fit their plans into the probable train of events, with alterations for altered circumstances, they often could not survive. Within this framework, the feat of believing that someone will come the day after tomorrow does not seem at all out of the way. To show that it is not possible would need an empirical investigation, not a conceptual ruling. Of course it is true that, amongst people, such feats are normally performed with words, and that these words make all sorts of far more ambitious feats possible. But that is quite a different story.

5   DESIRE, EMOTION AND BELIEF

Against this background, we can now look at the next rung in Frey's ladder, the idea that animals cannot have desires or emotions. This looks very odd, since these are just what animals are often accused of having too much of. I am sure that the analysis which linguistic philosophers have given of these terms is in fact being misused here. But this analysis itself makes an important point. It insists that desires and emotions are not just formless drives or urges. They incorporate thoughts.[10] The emotion of anger, for instance, involves the belief that someone has acted offensively. The emotion of fear involves the belief that there is danger, and so forth. In a general way, this recognition of the complexity of feeling goes back to Aristotle. But it has often been lost, and perhaps never fully used and understood. Recent versions of it, however, sometimes graft onto it the extra thesis that the belief must be expressed in words. Even within human life, this cannot be right, since the most inarticulate people can be angry or frightened without the slightest difficulty – indeed, strong fear or anger make most of us inarticulate. (The bystanders may be able to express in words the beliefs involved, but the angry or frightened subject need not be able to do so. Indeed, notoriously, he or she may not recognize the emotion itself for what it is at all.) The case of animals, however, is still plainer. Their emotions, like human ones, are recognizable by others because of the structure conferred by the beliefs on which they rest. Both their conspecifics and human beings with a strong interest in the matter – vets, mahouts, circus-trainers, hunters, grooms, ethologists and so forth – spot the difference between fear, anger and other emotions by observing a consistent set of reactions which makes sense only on the assumption of a given belief. If one asks what justifies this assumption, success in operating this whole range of alternatives is the answer. And with human beings, too, we recognize this direct expression of emotion through conduct as more reliable than its expression through words, when the two conflict. Wittgenstein seems to have accepted this wordless belief. As he says, 'the dog *believes* that his master is at the door'. We can see that this usage is correct by noticing that the dog may be mistaken. The person at the door turns out to be someone else. On this the dog, exactly like a human being in the same situation, turns away, deflated and depressed. (Where there is disappointment, there must have been hope.) Neither with dog nor human do we need words to reveal to us what expressive and interpretative capacities far older and far deeper than words make clear immediately.

6   THE IRRELEVANCE OF RIGORISM

As I have said, the value of linguistic philosophy need not be affected by recognizing this, because its main business lies with humans, who do speak. It often does not need to discriminate between the pre-verbal foundations of order and the more detailed refinements which are made possible by language. There are some topics, however, on which it actually ought to do this – topics where some attention to our sub-verbal ordering capacities would be very useful. An excellent book here is Konrad Lorenz's *Behind the Mirror*, which maps these capacities very clearly, and relates them to the Kantian problem of order.[11] For instance, Lorenz points out how Kant's 'category of substance' – the capacity to divide the world into continuing objects, and to separate them from their background – is needed and possessed by even very simple animals, far below the language level. A frog needs to see an approaching fly or bird *as* a fly or bird, not just as various abstract pattern-changes among the sense-data. Its perceptual apparatus is therefore adapted to make this possible. Similarly, on our present issue of emotion, an animal which is to survive and prosper must have its motivational states linked in a systematic and efficient way to its cognitive ones. Emotions and beliefs have evolved together; neither makes much sense without the other. This reinforces a point which seems to me already staringly obvious on the human scene. It makes little sense to attempt, as linguistic philosophers sometimes do, to give an account of emotions which centres on their verbal expression. Babies can feel emotions, and do not have their power of doing so increased when they learn to talk. The fact that animals do so too only underlines this point. A theory which simply rules this mass of evidence out of existence can command little respect. It cannot today make the excuse which certainly should be made for the remarks which I have quoted from the founding fathers of linguistic philosophy – namely, that the matter just had not come to their attention. In the last few decades, the complexity of animal behaviour and animal intelligence has, for good reasons, come well forward into the limelight. One of those reasons is an increased consciousness of the need to make sense of evolution. To suppose that speech could have originated among creatures which had no understanding, no concepts, no emotions, no beliefs and no desires is wild. Nothing in the serious purposes of linguistic philosophy requires this wildness, and it would be as well to get rid of it as soon as possible.[12]

These questions may seem somewhat remote from the moral issues which we are primarily discussing. And it is perhaps as well to stress that the architects of linguistic philosophy never intended their work to serve as a device for disproving that animals had rights – an issue which certainly did not occur to them. Does it, however, have relevance there? What does follow morally from an intellectual difference, especially from a large one? In Kant's case, what is the reasoning involved in saying, 'he does not fail in his duty to the dog, *for the dog cannot judge*'? This really seems to need explanation, because in a human case it would not work. Duties to babies, defectives and the senile, and to people too humble, confused or indecisive to be capable of judging whether they are wronged, are not cancelled by that incapacity. They are strengthened by it. Those who owe these duties become responsible for passing judgements on their own conduct which the incapable person cannot pass for himself.

Theorists usually separate animals from these human cases by distinguishing a special sense of *can* or *capacity*. All human beings, they say, are essentially capable of judging, and only accident prevents some of them from doing it. Animals are not. It is not clear that this works for all human cases, but even if it did, why does it matter? What difference does it make? In Kant's argument the difference is not practical. It does not excuse inhumane treatment of animals. It only alters the way we think of our action and the kind of reason we give for it. In doing this it seems to substitute a circuitous and unconvincing explanation for the direct and natural one which Hare gives, 'I wouldn't like it done to me.' Common-sense suggests that the duty is primarily *to* the animal, not to our own humanity or those we may later deal with. Much the same thing seems true of our duties to non-rational humans. These duties do not depend on our thinking, hypothetically, that these people might, if things had been different, have been able to judge us. They are duties to them as they are now. The only judgement needed about our owing them is our own. What would make this surprising, and what the objectors probably have in mind, is that it would not be true of duties of contract. These do need two contracting parties who share an articulate understanding of their bargain. But not all duties are of this sort.[13]

It is difficult to get any further with this argument because there are no other parallel cases. Those who are considered incapable of judging in this sense are all animals, and it is animals that we are inquiring about. Their incapacity is deemed to depend on their not speaking, which is – or was till lately[14] – a clear demarcation, making them outlaws by definition, without reference to their other faculties. What I suspect is happening here is that people start from a conviction that animals fall outside morality, and give this reason for it without seeing that it involves an unworkably narrow notion of duty. This we must discuss presently. It would be interesting, however, to work out the case of intelligent alien beings. In stories, they are necessarily often represented as being already able to talk, which puts them in business morally. Their mode of communication, however, would certainly not be ours. Good science-fiction writers rightly assume that duties could begin to arise between them and people, even before communication was established. Are we sure that whales and dolphins are not in this situation? If so, how?

7 RIGHTS

This is the really desperate word. As any bibliography of political theory will show, it was in deep trouble long before animals were added to its worries. On the other hand, it is welded far more thoroughly than *duty* to a legal and political context. It is used descriptively for a whole network of privileges conferred by law and custom, without implying in any given case any necessary moral approval. On the other hand, it still does have a strong moral use. To say 'they have no right to X' means – unless you explain that you are only talking legally – that they actually ought not to have it. Thus people with no legal right to a house or a pension may be said all the same to have a moral or natural right to it, which means that they ought to have it, and perhaps ought to have a legal right to it. Because the meaning of *moral* and *natural* here is not too clear, these phrases have become rather suspect of late, and are now often replaced by 'human rights'. This is no clearer. It has also the extra disadvantage of seeming to pre-empt without discussion the whole subject of this book.

I cannot go into these difficulties here, nor shall I waste space on citing the many arguments designed to show that animals cannot have rights. They are often justified, as far as the legal or customary end of the word's usage is concerned. (For instance it may well be held, at that end, that rights have to be explicitly conferred by a particular society, which can give them only to its own consenting members, or that no one can have a right who cannot himself understand and claim it.) But the other, moral end of the word's use is far less clear; indeed, some vagueness seems to be essential to it. And the relation between the two ends is not simple. It is certainly not just a casual ambiguity. In the first place, even at the legal end some moral connotation persists. Certainly lawyers are not professionally committed to justifying any particular right which they mention, but they do seem committed to justifying the whole system of legal rights in some degree, as a system designed for reasonable purposes. It cannot be conceived as only custom. In case of doubt, judges explicitly take those purposes into account. A judge's appeal to law and precedent is not mere historical scholarship; it prescribes standards. And the degree of respect accorded to law must correspond in general to its being supposed to have reputable aims. In the second, there are good reasons why moral thinking readily uses the language of law, why for instance even Hume, that least legalistic of moralists, found it natural to say that we are 'bound by the laws of humanity', although he insisted that the topic in question did not concern the state at all. A very natural way of relating them is to say that legal rights get their moral authority in the first place from pre-existing needs and insights, which they imperfectly formalize, and add the obligation of contract to this as something distinct. Thus, Rousseau derives the contract itself from the pre-existing motives of self-interest and compassion, and remarks that, since compassion does not stop at the species-barrier,

> by this method also we put an end to the time-honoured disputes concerning the participation of animals in natural law; for it is clear that, being destitute of intelligence and liberty, they cannot recognize that law; as they partake, however, in some measure of our nature, in consequence of the sensibility wherewith they are endowed, *they ought to partake of natural right*; so that mankind is subjected to a *kind of obligation* even toward the brutes. It appears, in fact, that if I am *bound* to do no injury to my fellow-creatures, this is *less because they are rational than because they are sentient beings*; and this quality, being common to man and beasts, *ought* to entitle the latter at least to the privilege of not being wantonly ill-treated by the former.[15]

8 RIGHTS, LAWS AND MORALS

The ambiguity of terms like 'right', then, does not just express a mistake, but a deep and imperfectly understood connection between law and morality. This is why eighteenth-century revolutionaries were able to exploit these ambiguities with such effect in their campaign for the rights of man. Obscure concepts can often be used effectively for reform in this way, so long as they are employed only on issues where their practical bearing is clear. They are like strong tools caught up and used as levers to remove a particular obstacle, without thought of their other properties. When new enterprises come up, however, different patterns of tension will emerge in the argument. Such concepts can then prove misleading or useless. Other ideas must be forged to supplement or replace them. The possible rights of man, woman, child and beast need to be considered from this angle, along with the rest of the French-revolutionary tool-kit, to which they belong, and particularly the idea of equality. We must tackle this formidable job in the next chapter. The actual word *right*, however, cannot, as far as I can see, be salvaged for any clear, unambiguous use in this discussion. It can be used in a wide sense to draw attention to problems, but not to solve them. In its moral sense, it oscillates uncontrollably between applications which are too wide to resolve conflicts ('the right to life, liberty and the pursuit of happiness') and ones which are too narrow to be plausible ('the basic human right to stay at home on Bank Holiday'). As many people have already suggested, its various uses have diverged too far to be usefully reunited.

If this is true, however, it seems very important to stop relying on it. In ordinary speech, as we noticed, to say that somebody has a certain right is a moral judgement; it means that something should be done about it, we ought to consider him. This implication is very strong and natural. Accordingly, to say that 'animals do not have rights' does not sound like a remark about the meaning of the word *rights* but one about animals – namely, the remark that one need not really consider them. Subsequently saying that they have some other rather nebulous thing instead will not get rid of this effect. The case is rather like that of someone who objects to using the concept of intelligence or talent for a particular group, because he thinks it vague or misleading, and who puts his point by saying that this group have no intelligence or no talent. The obvious meaning is so strong that he cannot put the point that way. He must reword it entirely.

In these two chapters, we have searched the tradition to find clear arguments for absolute dismissal. We have not found them. Descartes and Spinoza give us the dismissal, but not the arguments. People who feel attracted by their position will have to do the job for themselves. What we have found instead of reasoned absolute dismissal is a set of brief, casual but explicit demands for humane treatment of animals. These are linked, however, to conceptual maps which exclude them in each case from a certain important moral area. In Hume's case this area (justice) is anyway not the central one of morality. In Kant's case (duty) it is. Rawls officially considers this question not yet decidable, but his method commits him in effect to making justice look central. The question where the centre of morality lies is one of enormous general importance. The tendency of enlightenment thinking to place contracts, made by rational consent on a basis of enlightened self-interest between equals, at that centre deserves the sharpest attention. Whenever the spotlight picks out a particular moral area like this as central, things outside it tend to glide unnoticed into the shadows and be forgotten. Terminology, developed for central purposes, becomes unable to express them clearly. In such cases, philosophy must not just record and follow the usage of current theories. It must also be their critic.

6 *Equality and Outer Darkness*

I CAN ANIMALS BE EQUAL?

It is not till the last decade that philosophers have seriously and persistently extended the concept of equality, and that of basic natural rights, to animals. But they have done it now. 'All animals are equal . . . No matter what the nature of the being, the principle of equality requires that its suffering be counted equally with the like suffering – in so far as rough comparisons can be made – of any other being' (Peter Singer).[1] And on rights, 'Within an absolute context it is difficult to see how any of us, men or beasts, have any rights at all; and we certainly therefore have no rights upon them. In less absolute terms, any principle, or prince, that accords rights to the weak of our own species must also accord them to animals' (Stephen Clark).[2] Again – 'The right not to be tortured, then, is shared by all animals that suffer pain; it is not a distinctively human right at all,' and 'Whatever rationale is provided for granting humans a right to liberty, it seems that a relevantly similar one is available in the case of at least some other species of animals' (James Rachels).[3] Of course not all philosophers agree, but the disagreement has so far focused mainly on the proper use of words like *rights* and *equality* rather than on defending traditional dismissive habits of thought and practice as a whole.[4] Moreover the interesting term *speciesism* has been coined to describe discrimination against non-humans, thereby branding it as an offence against equality, parallel to racism, sexism, ageism and the like. Isolated writers had said these things before, but this is the first large-scale attempt to extend liberal concepts to the borders of sentience.

Historically, this movement was made possible by the other liberation movements of the sixties, converging with the increasing interest in animals which we noticed earlier, an interest which has for the first time begun to publicize the relevant facts widely. Books and films about wild life have told people something about the complexities of animal existence and its likenesses to human existence, and also about the widespread threats of extinction, which are themselves a new feature of our age, never considered in traditional thought. At the same time, books and films about such things as factory farming have been able, though with much more difficulty, to spread some information about how animals are actually treated within our civilization.[5] And again, many of the practices revealed are themselves new; tradition is dumb on how to regard them. The discrepancy revealed between ideals and practice is bound to bring into play concepts like equality and natural rights. This move, however, is not just a historical accident. Logically, these concepts demand this use as soon as it is open to them, because they have no built-in limit. They are essentially tools for widening concern, and concern, though it may attenuate with distance, is certainly possible in principle towards anything which we suppose to feel. Normally prejudice restricts it, but these concepts exist to break down prejudice, as they have repeatedly done. They are essentially destructive. Along with notions like liberty and fraternity, they work to dissolve the screens of callous habit and reveal hidden injustice. All these concepts are vague. All must be supplemented, once their work of revelation is done, by other, more detailed and discriminating ideas. But vague though they are, they are very powerful. They melt away the confused excuses given by custom, appealing from local laws and usage to the deeper standards required for change. Everybody who wants reform must sometimes use such concepts, but perhaps all those who do so are sometimes appalled at what they reveal, and find themselves retreating in alarm behind some ill-chosen bush. We must shortly glance at the record of these evasions in the case of the cluster of liberal, French-revolutionary concepts which are our present business. Repeatedly, even people who have used them well have set up crude barriers to halt them at various frontiers, notably those of race and sex – barriers which have crumbled scandalously as soon as they were examined. The dialectical road-block so far thrown up at the species-barrier is not less crude than these were, but far more so, because it has received even less attention. Anyone hoping to reinforce it will have to do the job over again from scratch.

This does not mean that there is nothing wrong with the liberal concepts themselves. They are notoriously obscure. It may well be sensible to halt them for interpretation and replacement long before they reach the species-barrier. But if one does not do this – if one puts complete confidence in notions like equality and natural rights – one lies open to Peter Singer's challenge. His opening chapter, indeed, is directed specially to egalitarians; it has the fighting title 'All Animals are Equal, or Why Supporters of Liberation for Blacks and Women Should Support Animal Liberation Too'. This does not mean, however, that conservatives on these matters can ignore the whole business. In our civilization, everyone who thinks at all has an egalitarian element in his thinking. We all need to clear up these concepts.

2   THE PROBLEM OF EXTENT

What, firstly, about equality? This is a rather abstract ideal, distinguished from most others by needing a great deal of background before it can be applied. Who is to be made equal to whom, and in what respect? Historically, the answers given have mostly concerned rather narrow groups. The ordinary citizens of a particular state – often a small one, such as Athens or Rome – demand to share certain powers of a still smaller group, such as their nobility, on the ground that they are all already equally *citizens*. The formula needed is something like 'let those who are already equal in respect x be, as is fitting, equal also in respect y'. Outsiders, such as slaves, foreigners and women, who are currently not equal in respect x, cannot benefit from this kind of argument. It requires a limited public.

The notion of equality is a tool for rectifying injustices within a given group, not for widening that group or deciding how it ought to treat those outside it. As is often necessary for reform, it works on a limited scale. Those working for equality take a certain group (such as that of Athenian citizens) for granted, and ask in what ways the nature of that group dictates that its members should be equal. This question is well expressed by social-contract language: what are its members here for? why did they form it? what, merely by belonging to it, do they agree to do? As we shall see, answers to this vary. But this variation does not affect the main point – namely, that the binding principle of the group tends to emerge as the basis of political obligation, and is easily extended to account for *all* obligation. This is no accident, for it is a central purpose of social-contract thinking to demolish a certain set of non-contractual moral principles – namely, those which tell citizens to obey their betters regardless of their own choice and interest. It demolishes these by applying a strong reducing agent – egoism. It asks, 'Why should I obey the government?' and accepts only answers delivered in terms of self-interest. There is much to be said for this. But when the same process is applied to other sorts of moral principle, results are much less satisfactory. Problems concerning the relations of the group to those outside it, and possibilities of widening the group, as well as relations within the group itself which are not considered as part of its egoistic binding principle, become insoluble. The notion of moral agents as equal, standard units within a contractual circle which constitutes the whole of morality is a blind and limited one. Contract has its place in morality, not vice versa.

It may seem strange and paradoxical to suggest that the notion of equality has these self-defeating properties. We will look in a moment at instances which show the paradox in action. It is true, of course, that the snags are not part of the concept itself. They belong to its supporting apparatus. But since some apparatus of this kind seems needed to bring it into operation, it is very hard to avoid them. The concept itself, as I just remarked, is very abstract, and can in principle be extended to any limit. In theory, when slaves or the like are noticed, the 'equal' group can always be extended to include them. But in practice two things make this very hard. One is simply the well-known difficulty about realistic political objectives. It is hard enough already to persuade the nobility to treat all citizens as, in some particular respect, equal. If we try at the same time to include slaves in the argument, we may well destroy our chances. Reforming movements which won't set limited objectives simply fail; they are not serious. So the 'equal' group comes to be defined as, for instance, that of free citizens, and habit perpetuates this restriction even when it is no longer needed. The other trouble, which goes deeper and will occupy us longer, comes from invoking egoism as the bond which is to keep the equal units together. The private self-interest of group members is often best served by keeping the group small. Where, therefore, pooled self-interest replaces hierarchical bonds, things may become worse, not better, for those currently excluded from the group. And if the whole of morality is in some sense reduced to egoism, the objections to this way of thinking become very hard to state.

3   EGOISM AND THE SOCIAL CONTRACT

All contract theorists have, of course, seen that there are difficulties about reducing morality to contract, and not all of them want to move far in this direction. The fervour with which they insist on reduction varies according to the violence of the emergency which they see before them. Hobbes, facing the bleak savagery of the seventeenth-century wars of religion, used a simple, sweeping version of contract theory, aimed at getting rid of all those numerous aspects of morality which he thought led to general destruction, and particularly self-destruction. He took the original respect in which people were equal, x, to be simply the power to kill. Everybody is strong enough to kill somebody else some time, and without a contract he may always do it. Since death is incomparably the worst possible disaster for each of us, that distressing fact alone is what makes it worth everyone's while to sign the contract, and equal protection of life is what they all gain. This self-preservatory decision is then the source of all obligation. For Hobbes, obligation simply *is* the fear of danger to one's life if a regulation is neglected. To make this doctrine work, the various duties and virtues have to be twisted into some very strange shapes; in particular 'the definition of INJUSTICE is no other than *the not performance of contract*'.

But it is impossible to extract from this tiny hat that large rabbit, morality. People expect and owe to each other much more than life and the means to life – certainly more than not-killing – and also much more than justice, even if justice is given a wider and more natural definition than Hobbes gives it. Human psychology is altogether not what he hopes for. People do not live in the future to this extent. They are (as their conduct constantly shows) much less interested in just surviving than Hobbes suggested, less prudent, less clever, less far-sighted, less single-minded, and much more interested in having the sort of life which they think satisfactory while they do survive.

4 THE IMPORTANCE OF FREEDOM

Hobbes, of course, wrote in an age of civil war, and has special reason to dwell on death. ('The Passion to be reckoned upon is Fear.'[6]) He therefore stressed above all the value of the state as a life-preserver, and described the outer darkness, the state of nature, as a state of war – a 'war of every man against every man'. Rousseau, in more peaceful times, took the life-preserving job as done and looked past it to other aims. He asked, now that we are surviving, what do we want the state to do for us? He answered that above all we want it to make us free and independent, to preserve us from every form of slavery. We want equality, not as an end in itself, but 'because liberty cannot exist without it'.[7] The degree of equality we want is therefore simply that which will make it impossible for anybody to enslave anybody, whether by violence, rank or commercial pressure. The emphasis has now shifted from viewing everybody as equally a possible threat to viewing them as originally equal in their capacity and wish for independence. (Thus Émile is to be taught 'to live rather than to avoid death' and to live in the present.[8]) That capacity and wish for independence must be explained. Rousseau explains them by an admittedly mythical description of primitive man as originally solitary and speechless, each person being able to maintain him or herself alone, wandering separately in the woods like bears, and hardly ever meeting.[9] He found it a standing paradox and tragedy that civilization had sacrificed this primitive independence to other, less crucial advantages.

In spite of its staggering implausibility, this myth of primal solitude has a solid moral point. It means simply that people – as they are now – are potentially autonomous, capable of free choice, wanting it and needing to have a say in their own destiny. Rousseau's remark that 'man is born free' means that people are not beings like ants, shaped by and for their community and unable to exist without it, but are true individuals who can live alone, and can therefore stand aside from it and criticize it. Émile, once grown up, is directed to travel, to see many societies and put himself in a position to ask 'Which is my country?'[10]

This native capacity and wish for independence is what makes it necessary that the contract shall be so framed that 'all, being born free and equal, alienate their liberty only for their own advantage'. In this way 'each, while uniting himself with all, may still obey himself alone and remain as free as before'[11] so that 'men who may be unequal in strength or intelligence become every one equal by convention and legal right'.[12] Any other kind of contract is a fraud. The contract now ceases to appear as a single area of light and safety, immediately surrounded by outer darkness. It is more like a patch of fertile country, chosen and fenced for improvement, but surrounded by a much larger expanse of very similar terrain, which shares most of the characteristics which make the enclosed land attractive. Social motivation is something far wider than political order.

5   THE NATURAL NEED FOR FREEDOM

Now to conceive the social contract in this way involves certain psychological views about the kind of beings who make it, that is, about human nature. *Nature* is here, as usual, a fruitfully ambiguous word, combining related views about facts and values. Why is independence so important to *Homo sapiens*? Why is it not better to live under a benevolent despotism on the lines of *Brave New World*? Rousseau's – or anyone's – reasons for rejecting this suggestion are in part factual, involving evidence about people's actual capacities and wishes, and in part moral, involving objections to certain ways of treating these: (1) People are not like ants, and (2) it would therefore be wrong to treat them as if they were. But neither these facts nor these moral judgements are derived from contract. They are the considerations which make this kind of contract necessary. Rousseau was always willing to appeal to distinct psychological and moral principles in order to explain why the contract had to take this special form.

In passing, it must be noticed at this point that bears are not ants either, nor are they cog-wheels. They, like people, are true individuals. The kind of liberty which Rousseau celebrates here is one which all the higher animals can share, and which all desire. It is outward liberty. It is not a rarefied, intellectual brand of free-will, depending on advanced thought and speech. It is a plain matter of not being imprisoned, bullied and oppressed, of having one's own way.

This outward freedom is what the self-governing devices of the contract are designed to secure. (Free-will, notoriously, cannot be produced by institutions and, if present, can survive in gaol.) Outer freedom does indeed give scope for a much wider inner freedom, which different species will use each in their own way, and for people, freedom of thought and speech will follow. But to see this, one must know the facts about the constitution of the various creatures concerned. And adaptation to liberty is a fact about the constitution of bear as well as man.

This appeal to natural facts – indeed to any considerations other than the contract itself – always causes political alarm, because the beauty of contract ethics is its simplicity. The contract myth – which is never regarded as literal history – is essentially a fence against arbitrary tyranny. It exists to make authority depend on the consent of the governed. Its main use is to cut out other, more superficial and biased, supposed sources of political obligation. It appears at its best in the opening chapters of the *Contrat Social*, where Rousseau makes hay of the jumbled religious-cum-historical theories which were used in his day to shore up the remains of feudalism. Rousseau's derision was a proper answer to theorists who derived the obligation of subjects from the right of conquest, implying that conquerors were entitled to perpetual obedience from the descendants of those they enslaved, or from the supposed biblical ancestry of kings. Nothing but the general will of the governed, he said, could relevantly justify government. As a lever for dislodging unwanted rulers, this principle is excellent. But where that is no longer the problem, difficulties crowd in. Now that we are demanding something more than mere survival from the contract, we shall need a different sort of inducement to obey the general will. Is that will infallible in promoting the liberty we now want, or can it make mistakes? If it can, must not other considerations besides actual consent be relevant after all? In disputes, might not the minority be right? What, in that case, binds the non-consentors to obey their fallible government? And – still more puzzlingly – what binds those who were never consulted at all, such as foreigners? What, in particular, binds women? All these questions except the last seemed to Rousseau extremely serious. He admitted the tension between the simplicity of contract and the complexity of morality as real, and he made tremendous efforts to resolve it. He never fell back on Hobbes's simple, reductive solution of eliminating one pole – reducing morality at a stroke to enlightened self-interest, expressed in contract. He saw conflicts about political obligation as real, because he understood that human psychology was complex.

6 THE DIFFICULTY OF LOOKING DOWNWARDS

The last question, however, struck him as merely a joke, and a joke in bad taste. It was perfectly obvious to him that women's consent to the contract was not needed, and he resented questions about the matter which could only tend to parody his own contentions, distracting people from the serious business of reform. Before glancing at the arguments

with which Rousseau and others have justified this dismissal, we have
to notice here, as a gloomy general feature of revolutions, something
which may be called the Paradox of One-Way Equality. Inequalities
above one's own level tend to be visible: those below it to be hidden.
This is not just a joke; there is a real conceptual difficulty involved. For
instance, readers of *Animal Farm*, encountering the principle 'All
Animals are Equal' usually take it to mean that all animals are, in fact,
equal. They are mistaken. It refers only to farm animals. In the first
flush of revolution, these animals do suggest, and uncertainly agree,
that rats are comrades. Attempts to act on this idea, however, peter out
almost at once, and the only other outside candidates ever named are
rabbits. Foxes, badgers, hedgehogs, deer, mice, voles, weasels etc. and
the whole tribe of wild birds, as well as everything smaller, are simply
forgotten.[13] It is interesting, though depressing, to see the same
principle at work throughout the liberation movements of the sixties;
each group of oppressed people, on sighting another, tended at once to
see it as a distracting competitor, not as a friend and ally. The story is
dismal. It is summed up in the reply of Stokely Carmichael, the noted
Black Power leader, to black women who offered to work for his cause
– 'The only place for women in the SNCC is prone.'[14] Equally and on
the other hand, nineteenth-century women, struggling against odds for
the right to education and interesting work, took for granted the cheap
labour of uneducated female servants. (It was still common, during my
own childhood before the war, for professional women to refuse on
principle to do even the simplest cookery or housework, in order to
protect their status. The group they identified with was defined by class
as well as by sex.) It is amazingly hard even to conceive, let alone to
fight for, serious widening of one's group at the same time as trying to
equalize status within it. This difficulty is a real limitation on the use of
the idea of equality itself and those ideas related to it. Another striking
instance is the development of democracy at Athens, where, with
infinite efforts, they forged and defended that *isonomia* – equality before
the law – of which, as Herodotus said, 'the very name is most beautiful'.[15]
This they did while their women were all incarcerated in harems and
their daily labour done by slaves. The American Declaration of
Independence, likewise, proclaims the proud belief that all men are
created free and equal, while explicitly excluding women and implicitly
(as far as some of the signatories went) non-European slaves as well.
We call this kind of thing hypocrisy, and no doubt rightly. But, as we
have already noticed, hypocrisy is not a simple matter. It is rather
seldom the full-scale Tartuffe phenomenon of fully conscious deception.
In most of us most of the time, it indicates conflict and confusion. To
call hypocrisy 'the tribute which vice pays to virtue' is not just to point
out that Tartuffe finds dissimulation worth his while. It is also to observe

that people cannot all at once become quite good, any more than they can all at once become utterly villainous. Havering and inconsistency are a condition of most human attempts at goodness. They are often best understood by giving them the benefit of the doubt – by viewing them dynamically as real attempts, and trying to see what blocks them. (This is not a defence of inconsistency, it is a suggestion about how to deal with it.)

In the cases just mentioned, the facts so strangely ignored are visible to us today, partly in the way that paint on one's neighbour's face may be visible, because we are not inside them, and partly because others have already pointed them out. The work which used to be done by slaves is done for us by machines, invented and still produced through a good deal of industrial servitude, much of it in distant countries. Hypocrisy is not, as people seem sometimes to think, an exclusive patent of the Victorian age. Nobody sees everything. This patchiness of vision is certainly a fault, often a disastrous one, but it is a different fault from Tartuffery. When a privileged group tries to consider extensions of privilege, quite special difficulties arise about being sharp-sighted. The notion that one has already drawn a correct and final line at which such extensions must end cannot be trusted at all. It is not trustworthy over animals.

7 Women, Animals and
Other Awkward Cases

I   THE INCOMMENSURABILITY OF WOMEN: ROUSSEAU

These four distinct problems on which I have touched – the position of
women, of slaves, of other races, and of non-human animals – have to
be considered briefly together here, not because their logic is necessarily
similar, but because their history is so. Inspected calmly and without
passion, these four problems might look very different. What unites
them is that they scarcely ever are so inspected. Admirable theorists,
who have been giving scrupulous and impartial attention to other
questions, tend, when one of these topics heaves up its head, to throw
the first argument which occurs to them at it and run. This habit
accounts for the sheer neglect of the animal question which I noticed in
Chapter 1; it has notoriously afflicted the other groups as well. On the
rare occasions when these theorists do not run, but consider such
matters more fully, their discussion often looks as if they had not
written it themselves, but had left their paper for the afternoon to some
weird secretary who wanted to discredit their doctrines. Aristotle's
discussion of slavery in the first book of his *Politics* is not just immoral,
but confused and helpless to a degree which is thoroughly out of
character. He writes like a typical Athenian gentleman of his day,
capable of seeing some difficulties and of expressing his conflicting
prejudices clearly, but innocent of the skills of abstract thinking which
might help him to resolve them. Hume and Kant, similarly, as soon as
they mention 'the fair sex', lose all sense of what their general style of
thinking demands, and simply recite clichés.

On this last topic, however, the really staggering example is Rousseau.
Far from avoiding it, he discusses it at length, repeatedly and with great
interest, but in the tones of exactly that pig-ignorant old pillar of crusted
prejudice whose arguments he so rightly exposed in the *Social Contract*.
Rousseau had described women in the state of nature as no less able
and willing than men to live independently. One would expect, therefore,
that they too would be signatories of the contract. But they are not. As
soon as society is formed, their liberty simply vanishes without explanation. The fine thought that 'all . . . alienate their liberty only for their

74

own advantage' does not apply to them. There is no question of their 'still obeying themselves alone and remaining as free as before'. It turns out that 'woman is specially made for man's delight'.[1] This makes it their duty to submit entirely to men – a duty which does not depend, as all men's duties do, on free consent. In its details, this duty of submission is no sinecure. It involves complete, full-time devotion to pleasing their husbands, and when possible complete abstention from all other social activities – an abstention limited only by unavoidable concessions to the mistaken demands of a corrupt society. Complete seclusion on the Greek model is best; in any case 'the genuine mother of a family is no woman of the world. She is almost as much of a recluse as a nun in her convent.' There must be not only complete fidelity, but an unspotted reputation; to allow suspicion to arise is as bad as to justify it, and actual infidelity is treason. Girls 'should early be accustomed to restraint' because 'all their life long they will have to submit to the strictest and most enduring restraints, those of propriety . . . They have, or ought to have, little freedom . . . what is most wanted in a woman is gentleness; formed to obey a creature so imperfect as man, a creature often vicious and always faulty, she should early learn to submit to injustice and to suffer the wrongs inflicted on her by her husband without complaint.'

Rousseau defends this endorsement of chronic oppression, so ruinous to his whole libertarian position, with a few remarkably silly arguments, centring on the frightful danger of cuckoldry. These arguments, however, presumably satisfied him. His public, therefore, might reasonably ask next, 'If these arguments are valid, why not educate women to understand them, and so secure their consent to their peculiar social position on rational grounds, as would be done with anybody else?' Women are not, after all, the only people who must accept some disadvantages for the general good; and if they are stupid, so are many men. This he never considers. He is most unwilling to educate women at all, and concedes permission to teach them a little about the world only because their company will otherwise be too boring for their husbands. Even so, it will be best if spouses do not see much of each other.[2] He takes it as obvious that allowing women to think will encourage them to revolt – which, indeed, it is, according to his general view of liberty. His demand is therefore that they shall do their incredibly onerous duty *without* ever seeing the point of it, from mere passive conditioning and a blind fear of public opinion – exactly the motives which he most wished to eliminate for men. ' "What will people think?" is the grave of a man's virtue and the throne of a woman's.' 'The man should be strong and active; the woman should be weak and passive' and that mentally as well as physically. About religion, being 'unable to judge for themselves', they must simply accept the creed given to them, even if it is erroneous. Altogether, they need not make choices. Sophie, who has been properly educated, 'knows no course of conduct but the right'. 'The most virtuous woman in the world is she who knows least about virtue.' Sophie has read only two books, and those by chance ('What charming ignorance!').

These views on education are all the odder because, in considering male growth, Rousseau had vigorously stressed that human potentiality is unknown, and must not be read off from existing performance. Men as they are have all been corrupted by bad upbringing. Reformers must allow for this and look carefully for indications of the very different beings which boys can and should become. Over women, however, he drops this idea flat, and describes female nature directly from existing custom – indeed, from the customs of the more depressing sections of the French upper classes. 'Women were not meant to run.' A woman is a being who 'has hardly ventured out of doors without a parasol and who has scarcely put a foot to the ground'. Passive, weak and proud of her weakness she can get her way only by 'contriving to be ordered to do what she wants'. Little girls 'are flatterers and deceitful and soon learn to conceal their thoughts'; they 'always dislike learning to read and write'. 'A man says what he knows; a woman says what will please.' And practically speaking, in spite of their primitive foraging ability, women are a wash-out – 'Woman, honour your master. He it is who works for you, he it is who gives you bread to eat; this is he!' A few pages later, he repeats almost verbatim parts of the libertarian manifesto of the *Contrat Social*, with its red-hot denunciation of slavery, and its promise that 'every man in obeying the sovereign only obeys himself'.

2 PSYCHOLOGICAL DIFFICULTIES

Now all this is not just a sad but exceptional case-history of self-deception. The significance of Rousseau's little disagreement with himself here is twofold. First, indeed, it illustrates the pathology of egalitarianism, the emotional pressures and temptations obscuring the subject. But also, and more constructively, it lights up real conceptual difficulties about equality itself, difficulties which would be there however calm we might be.

First, then, the pathology. Of course this would not be relevant to controversy at all if it was a merely personal matter. And it may at first seem that it is so, because Rousseau's life was so strange. He had good emotional reasons for talking in this way. He was a shy, diffident, lonely, self-made person with plenty of experience of life at the bottom of the heap. As orphan apprentice, servant and destitute wanderer, he had fully felt the miseries of dependence. He climbed out of this slough partly by his own efforts, but also by the patronage of several strong-minded, well-read, argumentative, aristocratic ladies, and of men like

Diderot and Baron d'Holbach, who could talk him into the ground. He was grateful, but all help wounded his pride, and increasingly the wounds festered. In middle life he began to see every friend as a patron and every patron as a secret enemy. In his private life – though seldom in his writings – his love of liberty grew paranoid, and he showed increasingly that grim twist of motivation which has wrecked so many revolutions: a resentment of tyranny which springs from a black desire to do the tyrannizing oneself. By way of compensation for dependence on his patronesses, he settled down with Thérèse le Vasseur, an illiterate and by his own account almost half-witted woman who, though often deceiving him, never openly opposed his wishes, and allowed him, though unwillingly, to dump their five children at birth in the Foundling Hospital. The terror of more formidable ladies, however, remained, and the last book of *Émile*, from which I have been quoting, fairly crackles with spite, resentment and fear. Inert though they may be, women, it seems, are still a horrible menace. If female modesty were relaxed, 'the men, tyrannized over by the women, would at last become their victims, and would be dragged to their death without the least chance of escape'. Women ought to accept their servitude because 'it is only fair that woman should bear her share of the ills she has brought upon men', and 'Women are more responsible for men's follies than men are for women's.'[3]

Now this sort of thing, and the rest of Rousseau's tirade, is not just part of his personal case-history, because the attitudes to women expressed here have often been expressed elsewhere, and relied on seriously by people resisting reform. It *is* part of a case-history in being much more extreme than the views which most people – and indeed even Rousseau himself – live by most of the time. In itself, it is neurotic. But when a topic is not thought out clearly, people characteristically deal with it by leaping from one to another of a mixed set of attitudes, some of them often distinctly crazy. Crazy views not properly exorcized by thought are held in reserve, ready to fall back on if more reasonable ones become inconvenient. Chronic ambivalence paralyses thought. Thus the gradual emancipation of women during the nineteenth century was constantly blocked by openly irrational fears and resentments similar to Rousseau's. His unbalanced character did not produce his misogyny; it only intensified and made him openly express an attitude which others shared. More cautious theorists, who undoubtedly also shared it, held their tongues, but attempts at practical reform always released the bats from the belfry.

Anyone who thinks it quite obvious that equality extends to, and stops exactly at, the species barrier should read the literature of women's emancipation as well as that of colonialism. Thus a member of parliament, opposing the Married Women's Property Bill of 1868, denounced the proposal that a wife should own any property as introducing 'a novel principle of civil equality between the sexes' and creating 'a factitious, an artificial and an unnatural equality between man and woman'.[4] (The measure was thrown out, and did not become law till 1882.) About colonialism, it is striking how often the European emigrants to places like America and Australia disregarded the claims of the local inhabitants, although they themselves had often left home to escape the tyrannies and inequalities of Europe, and held explicit views opposed to these. Their attitude was, in practice, all the same in general often that of the Brazilian farmer who told a journalist investigating the native problem, 'Indians and pigs are the same thing. If either one comes on my land, I don't think twice – I kill them.'[5]

3   THE SYMBOLIC MEANING OF WOMEN AND ANIMALS

The difficulty here is not just the political one, that to extend privilege is to part with power. It also concerns symbolism. The fear of women is a fear of the impulses they arouse and the forces they stand for. They are not seen as actual, limited beings in the world with their own wishes and problems, but as fantasy figures, angels or witches, elementals with all the spiritual power of whatever emotions they represent. The ground of Rousseau's panic is clearly that, for him, a woman is an internal part of a man's life. How can that part assume independence and start to act on its own? The resulting terror is like that of Frankenstein when the monster first peers through his curtains. It makes a far deeper and more intimate danger than that of surrendering some external, political power. Female suffrage did not make much difference politically, but its symbolic importance was enormous. External power is important here only in so far as it shapes institutions which work to protect the fantasies of the dominant group. Had women been that group, they would no doubt have expressed their own fantasies institutionally in the same way. Realism, which is essential for everybody, is always slightly easier for subordinates.

Women, however, are not our main topic here; let us look at other sorts of symbolism. Here is Jung discussing how in dreams animals represent the passions.

This manner of representation is very familiar to the analyst, through the dreams and fantasies of neurotics (and of normal men). The impulse is readily represented as an animal, as a bull, horse, dog etc. One of my patients, who had questionable relations with women, and who began the treatment with the fear, so to speak, that I would surely forbid him his sexual adventures, dreamed that I (his physician) very skilfully speared to the wall a strange animal, half pig, half crocodile. Dreams swarm with such theriomorphic representations of the libido.

The whole use of words like *brute, beast, animal, wolf, rat, snake* etc. is steeped in this symbolism. It has enormous power, and deeply distorts traditional Western beliefs about the actual behaviour of animals. Very illuminatingly, Jung goes on to compare the symbolism of race:

> I have frequently observed in the analysis of Americans that certain repressed complexes, i.e. repressed sexuality, are represented by the symbol of a Negro or an Indian; for example, where a European tells in his dream 'Then came a ragged, dirty individual', for Americans and for those who live in the tropics, it is a Negro.[6]

Both ordinary speech and literature tell the same tale. This sinister symbolism is of course balanced by an idealization, that of the Noble Savage, which is actually also very prominent in the fantasies that Jung is here discussing. As in the case of women, ambivalence produces a kind of mental squint, splitting the idea of the alien group into compensating half-images, between which the imagination oscillates in an uncontrolled way. The same thing happens about animals. They, too, have often been held sacred and even deified. A severe monotheism has cut this habit out of our own tradition, but probably in most others some idealization is present to balance the alarm. Even in our own, idealizations exist, notably in the images presented to children, such as that of the traditional farmyard. But unless such pictures are brought together with their contraries and with the facts, to form a more realistic whole, they only contribute to the general confusion. As for what the sinister symbols actually mean, Jung very sensibly operates with a wide notion of *libido* which is not merely sexual, but extends, as he explains, over a range of powerful and mysterious psychological factors, not always evil but often life-giving. What they have in common, however, is that they are mysterious – that is, things not fully understood and integrated into a safe, conscious, daytime existence. They are therefore frightening, and symbolizers whose fright is, for whatever reason, sharply activated are likely to attack them in self-defence.

It is therefore always dangerous to be an entity which carries one of these loads of significance. Many human beings and also many animals quite harmless to man and even useful, such as toads, spiders and grass-snakes, have suffered a great deal from being draped with unsuitable symbolic values. Carnivores like wolves and lions have been viewed quite unrealistically as deliberate criminals, murdering wildly for the fun of it. The devil himself is seen as half-animal. Even creatures which, to the conscious mind, have no special distinctive symbolism, still always have the general one that they represent a vast non-human realm, in many ways alien to us and beyond our understanding. To many of us much of the time this thought is delightful, but it can also be seen as a threat.

4   DISTANCING DEVICES

Those who defend the treatment of animals as mere objects, antiseptically detached from sympathy, in laboratories and battery farms seem to be setting up a psychological defence against this vast and pervasive mystery. As a farming magazine put it,

> The modern layer is, after all, only a very efficient converting machine, changing the raw material – feedingstuffs – into the finished product – the egg – less, of course, maintenance requirements.[7]

Or, to quote a veterinarian,

> animals used in biomedical research should not be considered as mere animals but rather as standardized biological research tools.[8]

What does this mean? Since one cannot stop an animal being an animal, it seems to mean that we will change the symbolism, thereby blinding ourselves to the independent consciousness of the creature and changing our sentiments. But (as we saw in Chapter 3) what matters is not our sentiments, but the facts in the world, to which our feelings as well as our thought should be appropriate. Stephen Clark comments, 'Certainly sentimentality is our enemy; the inability to see the real, suffering animal for a haze of aestheticism, misplaced piety and emotional projections.'[9]

Admiration for science and technology seems to be invoked here to give the flavour of realism to a remark which (in the first of these extracts) is simply false. A bird is so far from being *only* a machine that it is not a machine at all. Nobody made it. Nor has it been rendered unconscious – which is what *only* seems to imply. (Compare the proposition that 'after all, a human being is only £5 worth of chemicals' . . .) The second extract, more cautiously leaving the facts alone, merely demands that the animals shall be differently considered, that is, their consciousness shall be ignored. But consciousness is not something you can ignore, as you might decide to ignore some symbolic value which had been conferred on (say) a particular place or stone by a cultural quirk which you do not share. It is a fact in the world, not soluble by emotional chemistry. Where there are conflicts, considerations of it may of course have to give way to other considerations. But this is something which needs to be decided openly by conscious thought. Mindless absolute dismissal, secured by stifling thought, is as disreputable here as it would be – and indeed has been – for the human groups we have mentioned.

5 CONCEPTUAL PROBLEMS ABOUT EQUALITY

Let us turn now from the pathology – the emotional temptations infesting the subject – to the solid conceptual difficulties involved by the notion of equality. The trouble here is that the kind of equality put into the calculation is always adapted to what the reformers, on any particular occasion, hope to get out. Equality, like any concept used for practical reform, cannot be left vague. It must be put in specific terms because it is used to resist particular kinds of oppression, to redress particular pieces of injustice. Each kind of oppression has its own public, and the members of that public are those who for immediate purposes must be deemed equal. Suppose that the injustice in question is the arbitrary eviction of tenants, or wrongful dismissal from employment, or the seizure of people's means of livelihood by creditors. Redress for this will rightly be claimed on the grounds that the victims ought not – any more than richer people – to be deprived of their subsistence. But people who do not have a home, or a job, or tools, are left out of this reform; it does not concern them.

This does not mean that the reform is a mistaken one. It means that all actual reforms are limited, and that the notion of equality can only be used *after* one has decided which limitation one wants, for current purposes, to impose. Trade-union negotiations give the clearest example of what happens when equality is pursued as an end in itself, without reference to context – and that not only in South Africa. It is always possible to find a group of 'equals' within which one's own movement will be upwards. The relation between those inside and those outside this group has to be thought out separately in relation to justice, which is a much wider and more subtle concept. When the notion of equality is successfully used in a more general way (as it sometimes was in Athens and in the eighteenth-century revolutions), its users still always have in mind certain particular kinds of unjust privilege which are currently oppressive, such as those of the hereditary nobility. Equality is then defined by birth – but only within one's own country, since it is citizen rights that are in question. Resident aliens will have only limited rights, and there is no general commitment to allow the immigration of foreigners. Moreover, since it is taken for granted that the effective social unit is a household with a male head, women are excluded because they are women, children because they are children, lunatics etc. because they are lunatics etc., and slaves (if present) because they are slaves. With all these reservations – which are scarcely noticed by the people at the right end of them – it becomes possible to make considerable advances towards general liberty and social justice; advances which may, in the end, indeed benefit everybody.

Could this sort of patchiness have been entirely avoided? It is no business of this book to answer that question, but I think we must doubt it. It is hard to see how a large reform could start at the bottom, if only because that is where the scale is vastest. The usual pattern is for things to be improved, with great difficulty, in a certain small area, and for people then to ask, could not this be extended? Thus the theory of liberty and democracy was worked out in Greece, particularly in Athens, with much hard thinking and painful local experiment. This requires some leisure, and leisure means privilege. It was then used to subvert many of the institutions which gave it birth, such as slavery. Similarly, Marx had leisure to sit in the British Museum, supported largely by Engels on the proceeds of his clothing-factory, using the books written by many generations of those similarly privileged, in his efforts to change the world. Gandhi and others may well be right in saying that this kind of fact is essentially sinister, and poisons all reform. But it is hard to see how to escape it entirely. What matters is that we do not allow the chance limitations to become part of the system. It is the destiny of any real reformer to be transcended, to have his insights applied in ways which would never have occurred to him, and so eventually to look, to a superficial observer, rather small-minded.

6   THE IMPORTANCE OF THE UNNOTICED BACKGROUND

Let us stand back now to consider more generally what has emerged about the notion of equality. Both its strength and its weakness as a tool of reform depend (I have suggested) on its applying only to a limited, chosen group. To be in a position to demand equality, one must already have picked on a certain area of unfair privilege which one wants, and can hope, to remedy. Indefinite proposals are unreal; practical objectives must be limited. The notion of equality is useful because it has both the kind of versatility and the kind of rigidity needed for this purpose. It is flexible in that it can be variously applied. There are many respects in which the unfortunate can be shown to be equal to the fortunate. By choosing suitably their group, and their kind of equality, innovators can forcibly display the need for reform. The notion is rigid, on the other hand, in absolutely implying a frontier. It allows of no degrees. Unlike the older ideas of charity, hierarchy, fatherhood and the chain of being, it has no place for relations to subordinate creatures. Those who are not equal in the required respect are excluded altogether. Thus, from the rights of man women are simply excluded by definition, because they are not men. If the older ideas were not there to succour them, they would have no standing at all. Similarly, animals are flatly excluded from human rights, often just by definition of the term *human*. Those who notice that this is arbitrary often replace the term human by another, apparently more intelligible one, such as *reason* or *self-*

consciousness. These terms, however, do not really change things because they do not have their ordinary meaning here. They are not treated as empirical descriptions, the names of observable qualities which might have degrees, but as marks of status, often with the explanatory tag 'what separates men from the beasts', as if it were absurdly obvious what this was. Empirical observations about the variety of intelligence or of ordinary self-consciousness among different kinds of animals are not allowed to affect them.[10] This happens because they are thought to be necessary barriers to protect the frontier which the notion of equality requires.

Now this notional frontier has indeed been used to very good purpose in establishing the rights of oppressed human groups, particularly in resisting such practices as slavery, colonialism, infanticide and ill-treatment of the deranged. But this is no sort of reason for accepting its negative aspect, the dismissal of animals. This dismissal does not flow from thought, but only from negligence – the kind of negligence which constantly besets reformers when they consider, in passing, cases other than those on which they are actively engaged. This comes out strikingly in cases where ill-used humans are described as being *treated like animals*. If we are told that they were, say, herded into cattle-trucks and transported for days on end without food, rest or water, or that they were kept in a cage without exercise for passers-by to stare at, or that they were hunted down and shot for amusement, we are rightly appalled. But there is no argument leading from the fact that this is wrong treatment for humans to the proposition that it is right treatment for animals. This becomes clear if we consider the earlier cases where the rights of women or poor citizens were defended by insisting that they were not slaves. Nothing follows about whether it is right that slaves should be so treated. This question is simply not being asked. The lit area proposed for reform, on which the notion of equality asks us to concentrate, is always and by its nature surrounded by an area of outer darkness which we ignore. In principle there is nothing to stop us directing our spotlight onto it when we are ready to move on. But notions like equality, rights and even justice tend to imprison our attention in the area which has now become familiar.

7 THE AREA OF CONTRACT

Contract is another notion which has great force in making this imprisonment seem natural and inevitable. We must examine it next. What does it really mean?

Contract is of course a myth. We can understand it in two ways. It may stand simply for the existing body of law and custom. In this case it has the advantage of being explicit and definite, but it cannot be assumed to be right, nor to include the whole of morality. It does not help us for reform.

Alternatively, it may stand for something much wider, deeper and more notional – for an ideal area of unspoken trust and agreement, which all laws and customs only imperfectly formalize and express. In this case it can be used for reform, and since it very frequently has been so used, this must be the meaning appropriate to it. But what guidance does it give us?

Contract has two elements, reciprocity and speech. Let us look at them separately.

1. *Reciprocity.* The model of a literal, commercial contract – an agreement made between fully responsible, rational agents, solely to promote their mutual advantage – is an attractive one because it is so clear. Politically, it has been very useful in a certain small but crucial job – namely, to discredit the claims of rulers who were not worth their cost to those they ruled. But as we have seen, it cannot possibly be extended to cover the whole of morality. To speak only of a few central cases, morality must include many duties to the helpless, such as those to babies and defectives. These are real duties, not some shaky sort of quasi-duty, and they are owed *to them* as they are now, not to the wily contractors that they may some day become. The position is *not* that which obtains when a Mafia boss is ill, and his subordinates wonder whether it will be worth their while to carry out his orders on the chance of his recovery or not. In the case of the incurable, this is obvious. But even in that of normal children, the bargaining model is much less appropriate than people tend to think. Parental duty is not so much reciprocal as transitive – passed on. The parents pay to their children the care which they received from their own parents, who received it from theirs, and so on indefinitely. The main payment is never back to the giver, but always forward to the next receiver. Certainly children come to owe a duty to their parents too, and in normal cases do repay them for their care. But this duty is different in kind, and the situation is never the symmetrical one of a commercial bargain. Had people been as carefully calculating and self-absorbed as Hobbes suggested, they would only bring up children when it was worth their while to have their support in old age. With the very long period of dependence of children in our species, this would seldom happen. Mime does it to Siegfried in Wagner's *Ring*, but he had a special reason for it, and his behaviour is not at all like that of a real parent. Again, it is true that once children are there, bargains are struck with them, but this will never make bargaining the essence of the business. We need only look at the way in which parents often care for an incurably handicapped child to see this. Nor is it surprising. Parental motives and duties should not puzzle anyone except a dogmatic egoist, and dogmatic egoists need only look

round at the general parental behaviour of birds and mammals to see the implausibility of their dogma. Good egoists make bad parents, and in species where there is any parental care at all, natural selection soon extinguishes their line. The long childhood now characteristic of our species has been made possible only because selection has favoured the emotional constitution which leads to very generous parenting.

The ideal area of unspoken trust is not, then, confined to reciprocity. It allows of binding duties to non-reciprocators. At what limit, then, does it stop? Must it, as many people suggest, be confined to language-users? This brings us to our second topic:

2. *Speech*. Speech is often linked to contract in a remarkably naïve way. Thus Hobbes remarks that

> To make covenants with bruit Beasts, is impossible, because, not understanding our speech, they understand not, nor accept of, any translation of Right, nor can translate any Right to one another; and without mutual acceptation, there is no Covenant.[11]

Neither, he consistently adds, can we make covenants with God, unless he will talk to somebody, 'for otherwise we know not whether our Covenants be accepted or not'.

But on this line we could not use tacit agreements at all. Contract could only cover existing explicit law; we could not even extend it to include unformulated custom. The powerful myth of a *hidden* under-lying agreement vanishes. The weakness of this attitude to language is very tellingly exposed when Hobbes comes to consider the question of sanctions, and declares that 'Covenants without the sword are but words, and of no strength to secure a man at all.'[12] Words alone, as he sees, have no force. But it must be added that words accompanied only by swords are no better. Sword-wavers have to sleep and eat and go about their daily business; they have backs, and, as Hobbes noticed, it is not physically hard to kill somebody if you can choose your moment. What makes it possible for the words to produce safety is basic trust. Swords only reinforce this in awkward cases. Were it not instinctive in the species, it could not possibly be produced by self-interest, however enlightened. Solitary creatures such as bears may not have it, but primates, like all other social creatures, do. No such creature passes its life in a posture of constant defence. Remarkably enough, Hobbes admits this for other animals.

> It is true that certain living creatures, as Bees, and Ants, live sociably one with another . . . and yet have no other direction than their particular judgments and appetites, nor speech, whereby one of them can signifie to another what he thinks expedient for the common benefit.[12]

Why then (the objector may ask) cannot human beings do the same?

Hobbes gives two answers, of which the first is admirable and the second false. The first is that creatures without speech cannot disagree in the same way as articulate ones. Not having the problem of widely discordant expressed opinions, they do not need the solution of explicitly reasoned agreements. This is correct, and here the idea of covenant is simply that of developed thought and language. The second, however, is that animals are different from men emotionally, in ways which make it impossible for them to quarrel at all. Competition for dominance, says Hobbes, is confined to the human race. 'Men are continually in competition for Honour and Dignity, which these creatures are not . . . irrational creatures cannot distinguish between *injury* and *Damage*, and therefore, as long as they be at ease, they are not offended with their fellows.' Now whatever truth there may be in this for the social insects, there is none for social mammals and birds. (Insect analogies have in fact been very misleading here; they are much more remote than they appear.) Dominance hierarchies, established through controlled competition, are essential to mammal and bird societies, and in them deliberate attack is perfectly well distinguished from accidental damage. (No doubt this is not a matter of making moral judgements, but it does not have to be; it is quite sufficient to cause offence in the one case and not in the other.) They would therefore be in 'a constant state of war of all against all' were it not that these quarrel-making tendencies are more than balanced by affection and a strong emotional tendency to basic trust. Fighting occurs in cases of doubt to settle positions in the dominance hierarchy, but once settled, these are usually kept without further conflict.

Thus we now know – as Hobbes did not – that people are descended from social creatures already provided both with contentiousness and with a strong, subtle, positive sociability to control it. What Hobbes asks us to believe is that people naturally have the contentiousness without the remedy:

The agreement of these creatures is Naturall; that of men is by Covenant only, which is Artificiall; and therefore it is no wonder if there be somewhat else required (besides Covenant) to make their Agreement constant and lasting; which is a common Power, to keep them in awe, and to direct their actions to the common benefit.[12]

Such is the magic which he attributes to this power, that the agreement it produces will be

more than Consent or Concord, it is a reall Unitie of them all, in one and the same person, made by Covenant of every man with every man . . . This is the generation of that great LEVIATHAN –

the state. But this feat is entirely incredible. For Hobbes, fear is strong enough to weld into an unnatural unity those hard, impenetrable, essentially solitary and unweldable social atoms which he takes people to be. And when ordinary fear cools – as it must – the words of the covenant are able, by some strange spell, to maintain its effect, to control people in the same way that the sword would, if it were held perpetually before them.

8 EXCESSIVE CLAIMS FOR LANGUAGE

This idea is not just of historical interest. Hobbes's view of language as a force which can operate on its own, understandable without reference to the emotional constitution which makes it work, is still with us. In fact it is increasingly active today; we have already glanced at its contemporary form. Here we are only concerned with the irrelevance of language to traditional notions of contract. What Hobbes means by 'covenant' (which is his word for contract) has actually nothing to do with words at all. It is the tacit trust and good-will which subjects pay to their accepted rulers, and Hobbes is merely insisting that they have good reason to pay it. Nothing that he says shows that this friendly trust differs in kind from that which unites sheep-dog and shepherd, or guide-dog and blind owner, nor from that between subordinate apes or wolves and their leader. It is not produced only by danger, but is simply one aspect of the general trust and good-will which people, no less than wolves, naturally pay to those around them, except when something special frightens or annoys them. This basic trust cannot depend on language, since it is found in quite small babies, both towards their elders and towards each other, and between people who do not speak, or even do not know each other's language. Of course it is not strong enough alone to maintain peace, even on a small scale, let alone on a large one. It needs to be supplemented by all sorts of deliberate choices and agreements, in which indeed speech is vital. And these are Hobbes's main business. But if these more detailed agreements were really artificial – if they did not grow out of and express a pre-existing general tendency to trust – they could never be made at all. This is no remote supposition. It is something which constantly emerges in ordinary life when words and intentions are at variance. Somebody whose intentions are in fact deeply untrustworthy will often find it hard to get his words accepted, no matter how correct they are, while somebody trustworthy, but clumsy and inadequate in speech, may be accepted readily. Alien beings, if they were provided only with a typed transcript of the words used in human negotiations, would make a terrible mess of interpreting them. Non-verbal cues give an absolutely essential context.

The perspective on communication which I suggest here is the exact opposite of that assumed in some recent discussions of speech. These take fully articulate language – and, for choice, correctly printed language asserting propositions at that – as the norm of human communication. They are not much interested in exclamations, commands, slang, and casual chatter, and treat non-verbal communication as a negligible island of occasional exceptions in a sea of print. For certain purposes things can be looked at that way. But a glance round shows the error of proportion. The sea of print – so overwhelming when one is afloat on it – is actually just a lake, surrounded by a vast hinterland of non-verbal communication.[13] To look at it another way, what matters about people cannot be merely their ability to speak articulately. It must be what speech reveals, and what makes speech possible. Mere not-speaking cannot therefore be enough to rule animals out of consideration.

Thus the outer darkness which seems to surround contract turns out – again – to be a function of our attention, not something real and intrinsic to the subject. Agreements, both spoken and unspoken, can obviously add to our duties, or give them a special shape. But they cannot possibly contain them all. There are always outsiders. The absence of agreement with animals cannot, even if it is real, give ground for absolute dismissal.

8 Sentience and Social Claims

Let us consider now what happens if we stop treating the species-barrier as crucial, and instead treat all sentient beings as inside the moral community. Jeremy Bentham, starting of course from a thoroughly non-religious and Utilitarian standpoint, put the case for doing this. (He refers to the French because they had just abolished slavery in their colonies.)

> The day *may* come when the rest of the animal creation may acquire those rights which never could have been withholden from them but by the hand of tyranny. The French have already discovered that the blackness of the skin is no reason why a human being should be abandoned without redress to the caprice of a tormentor. It may one day come to be recognized that the number of the legs, the villosity of the skin, or the termination of the *os sacrum* [he means fur or tail] are reasons equally insufficient for abandoning a sensitive being to the same fate. What else is it that should trace the insuperable line? Is it the faculty of reason, or perhaps the faculty of discourse? But a full-grown horse or dog is beyond comparison a more rational, as well as a more conversable animal, than an infant of a day or a week, or even of a month, old. But suppose they were otherwise, what would it avail? The question is not, Can they *reason*? nor Can they *talk*? but Can they *suffer*?[1]

We have seen that arguments like this must be taken seriously. They cannot be rejected *a priori*, without examination, because they go beyond the social contract notion of ethics. Taken narrowly, that notion deals only with a limited area of life and tells us nothing about what should happen beyond its borders. Taken widely, it covers the area of trust, which certainly does not stop at the species-barrier. And even that need not be the whole area of moral concern. As for the notion of equality, its blanks can legitimately be filled in in various ways. On the face of things, the way in which Peter Singer (following Bentham) proposes to fill them in makes perfectly good sense. He suggests that 'no matter what the nature of the being, the principle of equality requires that its suffering be counted equally with the like suffering – in so far as rough comparisons can be made – of any other being'.[2] We will examine the rough comparisons later. Let us see now what follows if we do extend social consideration in this way to the boundary of sentience, rather than just to the species-barrier.

We had better get out of the way at once two mistaken consequences which may seem to follow from this move, but do not.

The first mistake is that the interests of all conscious beings would now have equal weight, leaving us with no way of choosing between the suffering of humans and locusts or dogs and tapeworms. Singer's principle speaks of 'the like suffering'. As nervous systems grow progressively more complex throughout the animal kingdom, it is perfectly reasonable on disinterested grounds to suppose that the capacity both for suffering and enjoyment also expands. There are many detailed cases in which we can check this. For instance, we can see how social birds and mammals are upset by solitude, or by the removal of their young, which would have no effect at all on simpler creatures, and how the power to remember and anticipate trouble, which is a speciality though not a monopoly of humans, can increase its impact. Singer's principle, in fact, does not work by putting all cases on a dead level, but, like the principle of 'equal pay for equal work' or 'equal help for equal need', by supplying a reasoned instead of an arbitrary scale for variation. This is, as it happens, the way in which equality principles usually do work; they exist to produce the right inequalities rather than to flatten everything out. The slogan 'all animals are equal' is thus not actually misleading, any more than 'all workers are equal' would be, if used to summarize the principles just mentioned. It does not, as I think the slogan of 'speciesism' does, indicate a confused concept. It only tends, as perhaps all political slogans do, to look at first sight as if it promised rather more than it does. Singer's detailed arguments are much better than his slogans, and should be used to interpret them.

2   SOCIAL AND ECOLOGICAL CLAIMS

The second mistake is the idea that, if concern extends to the boundary of sentience, it must necessarily stop there, making it impossible for us to care for such things as trees and forests, grasses, rivers and mountains. Sentience is important because of the very dramatic difference it makes in the kind of needs which creatures have, and the kind of harm which can be done to them. The duty which we can owe to a particular being capable of suffering and enjoyment must centre on those capacities. It therefore takes a different form from any duty we may have for example to a redwood, or to the species of redwoods. Our duties to swarms of very small or distant animals, or to whole species, seem to be partly of the ecological sort, resembling in many ways our duty to plants, but they can also have a social element of response to consciousness. People concerned to stress one of these sorts of duty have not always noticed how distinct they are, and have wasted some energy putting them in competition. I have therefore marked this difference by calling the first sort of claims social and the others ecological. Both sorts seem quite real, and, since habitat is so important to animals, they converge much more often than they conflict. There are, of course, cases where they do conflict, and we must consider them seriously. This clash is, however, no more surprising than other clashes between different sorts of moral claims, and we have to deal with it in the same way, namely, by working out the best system of priorities that we can manage, and not going out of our way to intensify them. Both sorts of claim flow from our being the kind of creatures that we are. As social creatures ourselves, we perceive and respond to consciousness in others in a special way. But as beings forming a small part of the fauna of this planet, we also exist in relation to that whole, and its fate cannot be a matter of moral indifference to us. We will consider later how this affects us, and in general what kinds of things can intelligibly be said to matter to us.

The special importance of sentience or consciousness in a being outside ourselves is that it can give that being experiences sufficiently like our own to bring into play the Golden Rule – 'treat others as you would wish them to treat you'. Nearly all of us would, I think, put that point to our small children if we found them tormenting animals, even animals with very limited nervous systems. We say 'you wouldn't like that done to you', and I do not think that this is a Father Christmas case of deliberate deception. We mean it. The Golden Rule does not, however, seem to apply to forests. If we have duties to forests, they are not of that kind. But there are in any case other sorts of duties, so this need not surprise us.[2] The point is that the Golden Rule (though not the only basis for morality) is very powerful. If we are to ignore it, good reason must be given. The point of the sceptical arguments which are being used today to suggest that we really know nothing about the experiences of animals, and can therefore find no parallels for the Golden Rule to bite on, is to supply that reason. We have already looked at these. They are not the sort of arguments which would occur spontaneously to anybody except those already committed to certain special sorts of theory, notably Behaviourism and certain philosophical views of language. Nor is it clear that even these people, if called upon suddenly to cut up a conscious puppy, would act as if they really believed them. It seems reasonable, therefore, to pursue the present discussion on the basis of ordinary thinking, which supposes that we often do know perfectly well when animals are suffering or enjoying themselves. (These two possibilities are, of course, linked; the reason for dwelling more on suffering than enjoyment is simply that the duties it involves are more urgent.)

3   CONSCIOUSNESS AND THE GOLDEN RULE

It seems to follow that there is a conceptual link between admitting consciousness and accepting some social duties. These duties find their general *raison d'être* here, and not at the point where we first detect reason, self-consciousness or speech. Of course these more impressive qualities impose important further duties of their own, but they are not the frontier of all social duty. This is not an arbitrary decision. As Singer explains:

> The capacity for suffering – or more strictly for suffering and/or enjoyment or happiness – is not just another characteristic, like the capacity for language or higher mathematics. Bentham is not saying that those who try to mark 'the insuperable line' that determines whether the interests of a being should be considered happen to have chosen the wrong characteristic. By saying that we must consider the interests of all beings with the capacity for suffering or enjoyment Bentham does not arbitrarily exclude from consideration any interests at all, as those who draw the line with reference to the possession of reason or language do. The capacity for suffering and enjoyment is a pre-requisite for having interests at all.[3]

As we have seen, a certain amount of purely verbal cafuffle has arisen about this. The word *interest*, like *duty* and *right*, is somewhat ambiguous, being fixed for some purposes into legal formulations, and extended for others quite widely to miscellaneous cases. Singer has therefore been attacked on the one hand for not seeing that only people can have interests, and on the other for ignoring the interests of trees.[4] Ecologists can indeed use the word in the second sense, when talking about the prospects of competing species, and lawyers do indeed confine it to the first. But this last habit seems to arise mainly because they are always dealing with disputes between people, and is further narrowed by the law's confining the term in general to interests in property.[5] It is not a general rule binding all uses of the word. In any case the point seems clear. A conscious being is one which can *mind* what happens to it, which *prefers* some things to others, which can be pleased or pained, can suffer or enjoy. Singer uses the word interest to sum up this range of capacities. This seems natural enough, but if the word is thought unsuitable, others can be substituted. What he is saying is that, for beings like this, the Golden Rule makes sense, and that it must therefore apply. Duties to consider them may for extraneous reasons be slight and may be outweighed by others, but they arise, and if they are to be ignored, some reason is called for.

4 CONSCIOUSNESS, VALUE AND SOCIAL ATOMISM

Readers may easily agree that this is the stage where that sort of consideration becomes possible, but may still be puzzled to see why it should also become necessary. The point is that where such consideration does become possible – where it makes sense – it is the right and appropriate response. To recognize the spark of conscious life out there *is* to see it as having a certain importance. This point about the spark has two aspects. You can express it from the point of view of the creature itself, saying 'since it is conscious, injury and extinction will be bad for it'. Or you can put it more abstractly, saying something like 'since it is conscious, it has value; if it is injured or extinguished, the world will be the poorer'. This second formulation, to which we must return, may seem the more mysterious, but for both formulations equally the same question follows – 'why should that bother me?' If we were the kind of impenetrable, essentially distinct social atoms which theorists sometimes take us to be, that question would be extremely hard to answer. But it would be just as hard in relation to other human beings as to outsiders.

5 WHY DO OTHER PEOPLE MATTER?

As far as human beings are concerned, the point about independent value has long been accepted, even within social contract theory itself in its less egoistic forms, and expressed by something like that slightly mysterious distributive principle which has always formed part of Utilitarianism; namely 'everybody to count for one and nobody for more than one'.[6] This is interpreted to mean that the Utilitarian aim of maximizing happiness must not be reached by making some people so deliriously happy that their pleasures outweigh the pains of those whom they exploit, and neglecting the exploited people altogether, even if the total sum of happiness which results is greater than that produced by a fairer arrangement. Arithmetically it does not seem to mean that, but then the detailed arithmetic of Utilitarian calculations is seldom clear and never conclusive. The principle was probably laid down in the first place as a precaution against the obvious danger of assuming that kings and millionaires count for 1,000, nobles and presidents for so many hundred, and so on down the social scale. But this does not tell us much. Apart from certain important external political purposes, such as distributing land, good things cannot really be quantified, and happiness above all would be impossible to quantify. The principle of equality, just because it is quantitative, has only a limited use. What then does it mean that everybody 'counts for one'?

The essential point does not seem to be quantitative at all, but to mean something more like the safeguard which follows from being recognized as an independent centre of consciousness – as a being with its own interests, which must not be overlooked. It marks a minimum of attention to which all such beings are entitled, and below which they must not be allowed to fall. This point has sometimes been made by saying that the equality demanded is equality of consideration. But this is still misleadingly quantitative. We are not called on to give equal *amounts* of time and energy to all human beings. We have to deploy our very limited powers selectively. The notion of equality does not displace intelligent selection, but exists to guide it. It prevents us from overlooking certain urgent claims which lie outside our ordinary interests. In the case of human beings, therefore, it is not a stultifying principle, spraying out an unmanageable infinite range of diluted equal duties. It supplements our existing principles of selection. Its first function is to point out certain definite duties which we would otherwise not see. Its second, which is subtler and wider, is to change the way in which we look at human beings in general, including those with whom we have no practical concern at all. It reminds us (in Kantian language) that they too are persons, not things, that they are entitled to respect because they exist as ends in themselves, not just as objects for us to look at or as means to any of our ends.[7] A person is not just a behaviour pattern, or a unit in the labour force, or a seductive body, or a nuisance. There is somebody inside there.

6   THE GROUNDS OF RESPECT

Now the conceptual link between *this* recognition and duty is fairly easy to see. Beings like this plainly do qualify for the imaginative identification needed for the Golden Rule. The question is whether they do that only because of exclusively human, rational qualities (as Kant thought), or on the wider ground of consciousness – the more general power of enjoyment and suffering, existing in a highly developed form in our species. This is a question about what we think important in human life, but it is not, of course, a question about everything which we think important there – merely about the minimum which entitles every human being, even the most abject and defective, to basic consideration and respect. Respect here does *not* mean admiration, but something more like recognition of the rights involved in independence. What licenses it?

I cannot do more about this large question here than notice it, and point out that the exclusive rationalist view cannot have a walkover merely on the grounds that for a long time it dominated the Western philosophic tradition. It does so no longer.[8] Nor can those people who reject it when dealing with purely human questions suddenly take it up as a quick means of by-passing the animal issue. Computers can, in a clear though limited sense, perform reasoning. Babies and defective humans cannot. Anyone who defines reasoning in a way that excludes computers is including consciousness in it. The next question after that move is how much consciousness itself matters, and why computers cannot exist as ends in themselves? It should be plain that the division into fully rational persons and mere things is impossibly crude. A crucial range of cases lies in between.

7 THE IRRATIONALITY OF DISMISSAL

Is there any clear principle which would prohibit absolute dismissal of entire classes of people, and still allow it for animals? I am haunted by a story in a biography which I once read of someone who, travelling as a passenger on an ocean liner, saw a couple of seamen fall overboard. He shouted and fetched help, but nobody did anything. When pressed, a ship's officer explained, 'We don't stop for Lascars.' Recognizing absolute dismissal, the passenger replied, 'Oh don't you? Then let's see whether you'll stop for me' and jumped overboard too. (All three were rescued.) The point is not that it is *never* justifiable to leave people to their fate. There could be other claims which made it really impossible for a given ship to stop. What stinks is the failure of thought and attention, the blanket dismissal of a whole class of conscious beings, without any attempt to weigh their individual claims against those which, in any particular case, actually conflict with them. Would this have been all right if those falling had been incurable lunatics? Is it really clear that it would be all right for horses? *Any* number of horses? The articulacy barrier is not consistently recognized in common life, since there are occasions when great trouble is taken to rescue (say) horses from burning stables, cats from chimney-pots or deer from floods. In trying to sort out this kind of inconsistency, we do not find a plain principle justifying blanket dismissal of animals, unless we are prepared to take a very rigid rationalist view of human life, which is objectionable on its own ground.

8 THE RETREAT OF THE UTILITARIANS

Historically, the rise and success of Utilitarianism seems to be due to its having made a determined attempt, however clumsy, to challenge the philosophic tradition's over-emphasis on intellect, and balance it by some attention to feeling. In spite of many faults and confusions, it has been able, by doing this, to lend immense force to humanitarian reform. It has expressed, and helped to generate, a far more sensitive attitude than previously existed to suffering in general and animal suffering in particular. Like many reforming doctrines, however, it was often too sweeping, and tended to prefer force to clarity. Philosophers have driven large vehicles through various gaps in Utilitarian argument, the most important of which from the practical standpoint is the narrowness imposed by its original hedonistic framework. Pain and pleasure are indeed very important for certain purposes, but they cannot possibly be the only things that matter in life. Accordingly, philosophers who support Utilitarianism today often withdraw to more abstract positions. What needs to be maximized, they say, is not happiness or pleasure or freedom from pain, but something vaguer such as the interests of those concerned. Many of them have also dropped animals out of their calculations. This move may well seem necessary if one is to keep the original Utilitarian confidence in arithmetic and aim at the happiness, interest or what-not of the *greatest number*. Cost-benefit analyses which included as equal units even rabbits or rats, let alone insects, would become impossible. We will have to consider whether Singer's hierarchy of subjective capacities gives an adequate priority-system for arbitration, or whether further principles, say of kinship or intrinsic value, are also needed.

In general, however, these highly abstract theorists have moved a long way from the original Utilitarian position. I am not sure that Mill or Bentham would have recognized them as their successors at all. It might be less confusing if they called themselves something else – interest-consequentialists for instance – instead. Singer, by contrast, is very close to the spirit of the classical Utilitarians, notably in his emphasis on the importance of subjective experience and in being an active reformer rather than just an analyst. His suggestion about the importance of sentience rather than species seems well in tune with that humane, non-dogmatic and far from crazy core of Utilitarianism, the intelligent extension of sympathy, which has become part of our ordinary morality, and has done much to correct brutalities (such as widespread capital punishment) long tolerated, for various reasons, by both Christianity and rationalism. Objections to his move will probably flow partly just from that general sense of unreality which we noticed in Chapter 1. I think that unfamiliarity does play a great part in this. If more serious considerations also underly it, they will emerge best from taking the argument seriously.

But there is also a worse difficulty about one part of Singer's discussion, namely the contention that any preference of our own species is nothing but a prejudice comparable to racism. He allows a principle of selection based on the varying nervous capacities of different animals, but refuses to supplement it by a further principle based on nearness or kinship, and dictates a sharp drop in the degree of moral involvement at the species barrier:

To avoid speciesism, we must allow that beings which are similar in all relevant respects have a similar right to life – and *mere membership of our own biological species cannot be a morally relevant criterion* for this right. Within these limits we could still hold that, for instance, it is worse to kill a normal adult human, with a capacity for self-awareness, and the ability to plan for the future and have meaningful relations with others, than it is to kill a mouse, which presumably does not share all of these characteristics; or we might appeal to the family and other personal ties which humans have, but mice do not have to the same degree; or we might think that it is the consequences for other humans, who will be put in fear of their own lives, that makes the crucial difference; or we might think it is some combination of these factors, or other factors altogether. [For instance, elsewhere he allows that a more complex life might in the abstract have a higher value, so that] it would not be speciesist to hold that the life of a self-aware being, capable of abstract thought, [etc.] is more valuable than the life of a being without these capacities. [But in general, he goes on,] whatever criteria we choose, we will have to admit that they do not follow precisely the boundary of our own species.[9]

Is the species-boundary really as insignificant as this? and is species-ism so clear a concept? We must look to this question in the next chapter.

9 *The Significance of Species*

REAL AND UNREAL GROUPS

The term *speciesism* was invented, as we have seen, for a particular purpose, as a device to winkle out exclusively humanistic radicals from an inconsistent position. It quite properly followed, as the night the day, the similar invention of the term sexism. *Ad hominem*, for their original purposes, both these explosive charges were well placed and fully justified. Self-righteous revolutionaries who expected their women to type the manifestoes and bring the coffee, but remain otherwise dutifully silent, could scarcely complain if their theory was publicly contrasted with their practice. Their position was not improved if they cheerfully consumed battery pork and chicken. We have already touched on the distressing subject of endemic revolutionary humbug. We have also noticed that the rest of us are probably in no position to get very bloody-minded about it. Humbug, like flu, is extremely common. But it is still dangerous and must be attended to. The more exalted are the principles which people put forward, the more urgently do their inconsistencies need to be pointed out. Moreover, the closer their critics stick to the original wording, the plainer does their point become. That is why the original term *racism* has proved so fertile, spawning in turn sexism, ageism, speciesism, and uglyism to date, no doubt with more to come.

For destructive purposes, I repeat, these terms are useful. But once the dust clears and the possible inconsistency is admitted, we need something more. To earn their keep, concepts must do more than suggest a surface likeness. What deeper parallels do these ideas show? In the case of speciesism, there appears at once a most awkward and damaging difference. Race in humans is not a significant grouping at all, but species in animals certainly is. It is never true that, in order to know how to treat a human being, you must first find out what race he belongs to. (Cases where this might seem to matter always really turn on culture.) But with an animal, to know the species is absolutely essential. A zoo-keeper who is told to expect an animal, and get a place ready for it, cannot even begin to do this without far more detailed

98

information. It might be a hyaena or a hippopotamus, a shark, an eagle, an armadillo, a python or a queen bee. Even members of quite similar and closely related species can have entirely different needs about temperature and water-supply, bedding, exercise-space, solitude, company and many other things. Their vision and experience of the world must therefore be profoundly different.

To liken a trivial human grouping such as race to this enormous, inconceivably varied range of possibilities is to indulge in what revolutionaries call 'patronizing' thinking – a failure to recognize the scale of difference between others and oneself. Overlooking somebody's race is entirely sensible. Overlooking their species is a supercilious insult. It is no privilege, but a misfortune, for a gorilla or a chimpanzee to be removed from its forest and its relatives and brought up alone among humans to be given what those humans regard as an education. If we ourselves were on another planet, among beings who considered themselves, and perhaps were, superior to us in intellect and other ways, we would have no doubt about rejecting such an offer for ourselves or our children. We must shortly consider why this is so and how far the objection goes, but the general point is that we are not just disembodied intellects, but beings of particular kinds, and to ignore our particular qualities and capacities is insolent. This applies, not only to species, but also to age, sex and culture, though the point is not so extreme and glaring in these cases.

2 THE AMBIGUITIES OF 'RACISM'

To deal with this difficulty about speciesism, we have to understand what the parallel between species and race is really meant to do. As soon as we attempt this, we find to our alarm that *racism* itself is an ill-formed, spineless, impenetrably obscure concept, scarcely capable of doing its own work, and quite unfit to generate a family of descendants which can be useful elsewhere. To say this is not, of course, to make any criticism at all of the cause for which it has been used. As we have seen before, very vague and confused concepts can sometimes be used effectively in reform, just so long as everyone concerned understands what they are after and makes it explicit by other means. It is when we turn from this initial, familiar context to use the words elsewhere that the trouble arises. Then it becomes essential to understand their weaknesses.

What is *racism*? It differs from *racialism* – which means the holding of special theories asserting the importance of race – in being concerned with practice rather than theory. It names the offence of treating somebody – for whatever reasons – in a way determined by race, not by individual qualities and needs. But this offence is too wide. It is committed in all cases of 'reverse discrimination' – that is, of redressing injustice by deliberately giving privileges to members of previously oppressed groups. On this simple definition, therefore, the state of Israel, various black power groups and other reverse discriminators are racist. One way to deal with this unwelcome conclusion is to treat the term as a neutral one, like *killing* rather than *murder* and *bargain* rather than *cheat*, and rule that there can sometimes be justified racism. But then the word ceases to be the name of an offence, which is what it was wanted for in the first place.

The alternative is to give it a more complicated definition. But it will not be easy to find one which will do what is needed. It does not help to say that racism consists in determining the treatment *only* by race, and that reverse discriminators are moved by historical considerations as well. This is no good because race prejudice also invokes beliefs about history. A concept like race never is used alone, but always because of beliefs about the other factors associated with it. And the individuals involved are still being treated in a way determined by their race, not by their own personal qualities and needs. Nor can we say that the essence of racism is discrimination which favours *one's own* race. This would allow judges or landlords of race A and B to oppress members of their own and each other's races, identifying their own interests, as successful persons, with those of the dominant group C. And it still blocks reverse discrimination arranged by the oppressed groups themselves, when they acquire a state – or even a neighbourhood – in which to practise it. The same disadvantage follows on a definition referring instead to 'the dominant or privileged race', since those who were formerly oppressed can always come to occupy this position.

This obscurity about reverse discrimination has done so much obvious damage to the cause of reform about race that the need for better concepts is probably clear by now. The term *racism* combines unthinkingly three quite distinct ideas – the triviality of the distinction drawn, group selfishness, and the perpetuation of an existing power hierarchy. The word *discrimination* re-emphasizes the first element. When we try to use these terms for other cases or even for race itself outside the narrow context which was originally taken for granted, the separateness of the three elements at once becomes clear.

In the case of species the first element does not apply at all. The distinction drawn is not trivial; it is real and crucial. This is also true, though less drastically, for age and sex. Certainly these distinctions have been misunderstood and misused, but they are real. One can be different without being inferior. Serious injustice can be done to women or the old by insisting on giving them exactly the same treatment as men or the young. The term *discrimination* probably cannot now be got out of this use, but it is not really suitable for the work at all. It still needs to be used sometimes in its familiar, favourable sense. To be undiscriminating is not a virtue. As for the second and third elements, they are of the first importance, and they need to be described plainly, not as part of a confused package. They are aspects of justice, and plenty of terms already exist for discussing them directly. Concepts like oppression, partiality, conceit, bias, exploitation, prejudice, entrenched self-interest, narrow-mindedness, privilege, self-importance and the like, with all the enrichments, both political and psychological, which they have received and are still receiving, will do the various jobs concerned all right. What cannot be done is to pile all these jobs into a single package and label it with a single word, such as racism or one of its derivatives.

3 WHAT 'SPECIESISM' MEANS

Turning then from the objectionable concept to the real work it is used for, what points does the word *speciesism* exist to make? Its most obvious use is to deny the contention which we have repeatedly discussed under the heading of absolute dismissal – the supposition that the species boundary not only makes a difference, but makes the gigantic difference of setting the limits of morality, of deciding whether a given creature can matter to us at all. Here speciesism corresponds to the most extreme form of racism, which takes the same line. ('Pigs or Indians, it's all the same to me' – 'We don't stop for Lascars'. A similar view seems to be held in many small cultures which use their own tribal name as the word for 'human being', and regard all outsiders impartially as fair game.) This extreme position, however, is obviously only the tip of the iceberg of prejudice, which can take far more subtle forms. Those concerned with melting it have in fact often been appalled at its capacity for persisting under endless transformations. The demolition of extreme positions by no means gets rid of all unfair habits of thought. If we want a clear view of the enterprise involved in removing prejudice, we need to consider what defines it. This, it seems clear, is unfairness itself, unreasonable bias. A belief is not a prejudice simply because it indicates a difference.

4 THE REALITY OF NATURAL BONDS

Differences, as we have noticed, can be real and can need to be respected for the dignity and interests of those most closely involved in them. Thus, the insistence of many minority groups on retaining and emphasizing their distinct cultures, rather than becoming assimilated to somebody else's, is no prejudice. Neither is a belief necessarily a prejudice simply because it points out some individuals, regardless of their merits or capacities, as objects of concern before others. The special interest which parents feel in their own children is not a prejudice, nor is the tendency which most of us would show to rescue, in a fire or other emergency, those closest to us sooner than strangers.[1] These habits of thought and action are not unfair, though they can probably be called discriminatory. There is good reason for such a preference. We are bond-forming creatures, not abstract intellects. The question which people who want to use the notion of speciesism have to decide is, does the species barrier also give some ground for such a preference or not? Is cannibalism just the same thing as meat-eating, or is there a significant difference? Leaving aside the moral crudities of absolute dismissal, how is the priority question to be handled? Ought the distinction which Singer recognizes in degree of capacity to be compounded by another which evenly down-grades all non-human species? If so, how far? Should a gibbon, if taken to have one-tenth of the emotional capacity of a human being, go down by one-tenth again on account of being non-human, and settle at one-hundredth of human value? Or is it a twentieth? To look at it another way, do the Quongs from Alpha Centauri, who are ten times as intelligent as ourselves, finish up at par for us, while for them we go down to one-hundredth or a twentieth of Quong value? The question about gibbons is specially poignant since there are tribes in Borneo who used to regard them as kin, and therefore to treat them with the same sort of respect that was given to humans – until they discovered that Europeans thought this mistaken, on which they began to hunt them like any other creature. At which point, if any, were they wrong? Ought an understanding of the theory of evolution to affect their decision? How does extra-specific kinship compare arithmetically with the intra-specific kind? Does the Quongs' alien origin make an important difference to their claim?

Attempts of this kind at detailed arithmetical estimation of claims seem to be quite useless. The results they produce cannot possibly be made consistent; they are usually also morally shocking. This, however, would be just as true if we were talking about purely human affairs. We cannot compare arithmetically the claims of those near to us with the claims of outsiders, nor indeed any other competing sets of claims. There are no definite quantities here, no units. But it still makes very good sense to say that some claims are stronger than others, and even roughly how much stronger. Less formal ideas of *more* and *less* can very well be applied, because these relations are constantly being worked out in the course of conflicts, which continually arise between various sorts of claims. We all learn to compare them, and to show our working.

5   WHY IS THE SPECIES-BOND SO SERIOUS?

Questions about the morality of species preference must certainly be put in the context of the other preferences which people give to those closest to them. These preferences do indeed cause problems. By limiting human charity, they can produce terrible misery. On the other hand they are also an absolutely central element in human happiness, and it seems unlikely that we could live at all without them. They are the root from which charity grows. Morality shows a constant tension between measures to protect the sacredness of these special claims and counter-measures to secure justice and widen sympathy for outsiders. To handle this tension by working out particular priorities is our normal moral business. In handling species conflicts, the notion of simply rejecting all discrimination as *speciesist* looks like a seductively simple guide, an all-purpose formula. I am suggesting that it is not simple, and that we must resist the seduction.

We have seen the difficulties which arise about its first element – the notion that all species other than our own should be treated alike. Singer himself, as it turns out, does not endorse this notion, since he takes account of their differing nervous capacities. What, then, about the more central component of speciesism, the preference normally given to our own species above others? Calling this preference a *prejudice* is treating it as unfair and unreasonable.

Now there are, broadly speaking, two things which can make a preference reasonable, namely value and bonding. There are difficulties about treating this preference as based simply on value. First, it is hard to find an impartial standpoint from which the judgement can be made. Second, there seems to be no attempt to weigh the value of the most evil, or even the least capable, of our species against the best and ablest of others. In so far as the preference does depend on value, it can be seen as a direct preference for the value itself, without reference to species. But it is not handled like this. It is automatic. Criminals, however odious, are in general granted a fair trial; it is only in extraordinary cases that people think it in order to 'shoot them down like dogs'. By contrast, the World Federation for the Protection of Animals estimates that, throughout Europe, some five million dogs are destroyed each year merely because they are unwanted, many by animal welfare groups.[2] Similarly, it is strongly argued that the lives of even the most miserably and incurably defective humans, even indeed of unconscious humans, or those anxious to die, may never be ended, that there can never be any question of 'putting them down' or even allowing them to release themselves. But primates may both be killed and experimented on freely. Degrees of capacity on either side of the human species-barrier are not allowed to affect this sharp divide.

J. B. S. Haldane, one of the great biologists of this century, pointed out that this raises real problems. As he remarked, such a proposition as

'John Smith is a complete fool because he cannot oxidize phenylalanine' discloses a relation between mind and matter as surprising as transubstantiation, and a good deal better established. On the ethical side, it raises the problem of human rights in a rather sharp form. Has a hopeless idiot the right to life and care, though he or she is not a rational being nor likely to become one? If so, has a chimpanzee with considerably greater intelligence similar rights, and if not, why not?[3]

Haldane is certainly suggesting the answer 'yes' to both questions. The solution of current practice, however, is very different for the two cases. As we have seen it is hard to defend this difference on rationalist lines, by first insisting on the high value of human virtue, reason and language, and then building out awkward extensions to cover cases like John Smith's where some or all of these things are simply absent.

6 THE STATUS OF NATURAL SPECIES-BONDING

Seeing this difficulty, people turn to a quite different line of defence and invoke bonding. An emotional, rather than a rational, preference for our own species is, they suggest, a necessary part of our social nature, in the same way that a preference for our own children is, and needs no more justification. We must look seriously at this position, in which there is, I think, a great deal of truth. The species-bond *is* strong, even outside the institutions which have been devised to protect it. The kind of reaction which makes Crusoe risk his life to save Friday from the cannibals really works. Crusoe was not at all a scrupulous fellow; he had killed and cheated and made his pile as a slave-trader. All the same, he feels instant horror at Friday's predicament, and accepts at once the claim silently made on him by the mere helpless humanity of a stranger. The instinctive bond is a real one. But, as Crusoe's earlier behaviour as a slave-trader, and indeed that of the cannibals, shows, its workings are by no means simple or reliable. Before trying to weigh its moral significance, we had better look at the facts about it.

The natural preference for one's own species does exist. It is not, like race-prejudice, a product of culture. It is found in all human cultures, and in cases of real competition it tends to operate very strongly. We can still ask, however, how far it takes us. Is it an irresistible motive, forcing us to dismiss outsiders from consideration? To prove that it was, we would have to show that the differential response to our own species was a far stronger emotional tendency than our differential response to our own tribe or our own children, because nobody doubts that our duty can sometimes call on us to subordinate tribal or family interest to that of outsiders. It would have to be so strong that all attempts to extend consideration to animals were doomed to failure as unnatural.

This is quite a different kind of point from the rationalist one. It is empirical rather than *a priori*. It rests its case, not on the articulateness or rationality of man as an abstract feature, but on sheer physical kinship and its emotional effect. It would presumably produce different conduct in many imaginable cases. For instance, rational alien beings would be honorary members of our moral community on the rationalist position, but not on this one, while non-rational human beings are a problem for rationalism, but not here. The suggestion is that our nature itself dictates where the border of morality shall fall, and aligns it once and for all with the species-barrier. What about this?

7 ZOOLOGICAL PROBABILITIES

First, it is plausible enough that our tendency to respond differentially to our own species is a natural one. All social creatures attend mostly to members of their own species, and usually ignore others. This can be clearly seen in such places as the Serengeti Plain, where large mixed herds of grazing animals live together in harmony, but do not acquire each other's habits, nor those of the predators who often roam among them. For any serious social purpose such as mating or fighting or gathering to deal with a danger, each normally seeks out its own group. This direction of attention (which seems necessary to the production of a viable species, standardized enough to use its own ecological niche) is partly secured by imprinting in infancy. So it is often possible for an infant placed in an alien group to grow up imprinted on it, and to imitate many of its habits. This infant, however, is just as bigoted about having only one species as a normal specimen. Even if many models are available for it, it sticks to imitating and loving its parent-substitute and those like it. If brought face to face later with members of its own species, it may transfer its allegiance to them, or more often reach an uneasy compromise between the two. But that is not the same thing as general neutrality.

The option of picking a mixed repertoire of behaviour from many species, of thinking all creatures literally and equally one's brothers, does not seem to be available. The tendency to species-choice as such does seem innate. Moreover, besides imprinting, there are always many detailed positive tendencies which are innate too. The adopted foal or duckling will never be fully integrated into its foster-species because many of the appropriate signals are impossible to it, and it has innate tastes of its own that will set it apart. It may live a reasonably contented life, and be unconscious of missing anything. But it will actually miss a great deal, because a whole range of its social capacities will never be tapped. A solitary duck reared among chickens will never get the clues it needs to perform many of its central behaviour-patterns. It shares some chicken activities, but by no means all. In some ways, too, it keeps getting itself misunderstood. It is therefore a deprived duck, just as it would be if it was kept away from water. Difficulties about mating illustrate this problem. Some species, even quite closely related ones, cannot mate together at all because of behavioural differences. Others can, but the hybrid offspring are not only themselves usually infertile, but unfitted for the full life of either species. Thus lion–tiger hybrids can exist in zoos, but would not have the neural co-ordinations needed for the very exacting, and totally different, hunting patterns of either species. They could therefore not rear young, even if they could produce them, so that if they survived in the wild, their lives would be very incomplete ones.

I think it is important to stress in this way that species-bonds are real, because unless we take account of them, the frequent exclusive attitude of our own species is hard to understand. There does indeed seem to be a deep emotional tendency, in us as in other creatures, to attend first to those around us who are like those who brought us up, and to take much less notice of others. And this, rather than some abstract judgement of value, does seem to be the main root of that relative disregard of other creatures which has been called 'speciesism'. I shall suggest in a moment that this natural tendency, though real, is nothing like so strong, simple and exclusive as is sometimes supposed, and has neither the force nor the authority to justify absolute dismissal of other species. A glance round the variety of human cultures will show that the extremely remote and contemptuous attitude sometimes taken in our own is neither typical nor necessary for *Homo sapiens*. But before coming to this issue, it may be necessary to justify the suggestion that the reasons for species-exclusiveness in humans are in general of the same kind as those that move other creatures.

8   THE DIFFICULTIES OF SPECIES-NEUTRALITY

To see this, we had better go back to our interplanetary situation. The virtuous and super-intelligent Quongs are offering to adopt human babies. Shall we let them? What do we need to know first? The first thing, I should guess, concerns emotional communication. Do the Quongs smile and laugh? Do they understand smiles and laughter? Do they cry or understand crying? Do they ever lose their temper? Does speech – or its equivalent – among them play the same sort of emotional part that it does in human life – for instance, do they greet, thank, scold, swear, converse, tell stories?[4] How much time do they give to their own children? Then – what about play? Do they play with their young at all? If so, how? Then, what are their gender arrangements – meaning, of course, not just sexual activity, but the division into roles of the two (or more) participating genders, throughout life? What singing, dancing or other such activities have they? What meaning do they attach to such words as love? Without going any further, it seems clear that, unless they are the usual cheap substitute for alien beings which appears in films – that is, more or less people in make-up – we shall find that the answers to these questions give us some reasons to refuse their offer completely, even if reluctantly. And these reasons will be of the same kind that applied to the duckling. A human being needs a human life.

Is this sort of objection mere prejudice? Zoology would not say so. It would back our impression that, for a full life, a developing social creature needs to be surrounded by beings very similar to it in all sorts of apparently trivial ways, ways which abstractly might not seem important, but which will furnish essential clues for the unfolding of its faculties. Are there any counter-examples which could show us humans as an exception to this principle because of our flexibility? Stories of wolf-children etc. are hard to evaluate, partly because the actual evidence is slight, partly because all have died soon after capture. It seems impossible that a child should be brought up *from the start* by wolves or any other terrestrial species, because the sheer physical work needed is beyond them. (Mowgli seems to have reached his wolves at about the age of two, which is still remarkably early.) If in this way the thing could be done, the wolf-person would, presumably, have mixed imprinting and have gained some foothold in both worlds, but would be lonely in both – would be excluded from many central joys, and would keep getting himself misunderstood on both sides. Certainly he might gain some kinds of understanding which would be some compensation for this. But the price paid would be terribly heavy – a far deeper variety of 'being at home nowhere' than that which afflicts people brought up to oscillate between two cultures.

A much better way of handling serious inter-species relations is described in C. S. Lewis's delightful novel *Out of the Silent Planet*. This shows a world where three quite different intelligent species co-exist. They live in peace, do business together and respect each other, giving the name *hnau*, rational creatures, to their whole class, and including under that heading, in spite of occasional doubts, the visiting human beings. But most of the time each keeps to its own way of life and its own preferred kind of country. When they do meet, they get on reasonably well, but tend to find each other very funny. They differ considerably in their habits and interests, admire each other's specialities, and do not raise the question whose life is best. This arrangement shows species-loyalty as a quite unpretentious emotional matter, a bond, not an evaluation. And it rightly suggests that it need not determine the borders of social intercourse.

9 LOYALTY IS NOT EXCLUSIVENESS

For we have to notice next that species-loyalty in social animals, strong though it is, is not necessarily exclusive. At an ordinary social level, creatures of different species are certainly often aware of each other, and are probably interacting quietly far more than we realize. (Would an observer of an alien species pick up all our own social interactions?) This background awareness becomes visible at once when members of one's own species are removed. Thus, Jane Goodall describes how, even in the wild, a somewhat isolated juvenile chimp finds a playmate in a young baboon.[5] And the thing is well established in captivity. For instance, if a grazing animal – horse, cow, donkey, goat or the like – is left quite alone in a field, it grows very uneasy and depressed. But if a companion of some other species is brought in, it cheers up at once. They often do not seem to pay each other any particular attention, but the bond is there, apparently much as it would be with a conspecific. More remarkable still, an outsider may be cherished even when one's own species is present. A clear instance is the well-established tendency of race-horses to become attached to some apparently unimpressive stable-companion, such as a goat or even a cat, and to pine if they are separated from it.[6]

10 SPECIES-BONDS ARE NOT INFALLIBLE

On the other side of the coin, we must notice that species-recognition does not necessarily lead to amity. The first attachment of social creatures is usually to their own group. Strangers, and even more strange bands, of one's own species are usually viewed at first with some alarm. They may eventually be accepted, but at least a period of familiarization is normally needed, and often some fighting, or at least sparring to determine dominance, must be gone through first. Chimps, who used to be cited as exceptions to this general rule, have turned out not to be so; their groups are indeed quite large, but they have limits, and outsiders do get sharply repelled.[7] Of course this tendency to exclude strangers is now rightly treated with some caution, because it was crassly over-emphasized by those who used to dramatize animal life as perpetually red in tooth and claw. But we have to take it seriously, because it illustrates a difficulty which is essential to social life. The more richly a social bond develops, the greater, inevitably, is the difference between those inside it and those without. Beings which treat acquaintances and strangers alike – as do those simpler creatures which merely go about in herds, without individual recognition – have no reason to be exclusive. They will accept, in their weak kind of acceptance, any conspecific who arrives, and for them, therefore, their species is the only real community.[8] But the more lively and complex creatures cannot possibly do this. Their attachment to their own small community stands in the way of wider bonding. There are always some tendencies which counter this exclusiveness, some roads to the acceptance of strangers, but their capacity is limited.

11 HUMAN NON-HUMANS

In animal cases, then, the species-bond does not exactly coincide with the area of concern; there are (as Singer rightly suggests) overlaps both ways. What, however, about *Homo sapiens*? A glance round the wide human scene suggests, on the face of things, that the discrepancy there is not narrower, but wider. On the one hand, even in explicit terms of language, not all humans admit all others as belonging to their species at all. The arrangement whereby the name of one's own tribe is also the word for 'human being' seems to be quite widespread. This can – though perhaps it need not – mean that outsiders are treated as 'only animals', notably in the two important respects of hunting them down without hesitation and rejecting with horror the idea of intermarrying with them. This attitude is part of the larger phenomenon called 'pseudo-speciation' – the tendency for human beings to regard their cultures as if they actually were separate species. Pseudo-speciation is what makes it possible for 'cultural evolution' to proceed so fast. Customs of all kinds are accepted by imprinting early in life, taken for granted as a part of one's constitution, in a way which makes it easy to go forward and make whatever new inventions are needed to supplement them. The price paid for this, however, is that people with different customs tend, at a glance, to seem like members of a different species, and so to be rejected. Of course it is possible to resist this process, but a glance around the world makes it clear that this needs a positive effort. Baboons, presumably, do not ask themselves whether the baboons of a strange invading band are really proper baboons at all, but people can ask this question, and can answer it with a no.

12 NON-HUMAN HUMANS

Thus the social community which humans recognize does not necessarily contain their whole species. But neither, on the other hand, does it necessarily exclude all members of other species. Here we encounter the wide and confusing, but genuine, range of customs which has been roughly lumped together by theorists under the heading of *totemism*.

Particular kinds of animals can be held sacred, protected, cherished and, most significantly, even viewed as ancestors. They can be worshipped as gods. They can be buried (as in ancient Egypt) with full human or super-human honours. Wives can be dedicated to them and mystical marriage-ceremonies performed. And offences against them can be resented exactly as though they were offences against tribal members. (Thus it is said that the origin of the Mau-Mau movement in Kenya was an incident when a white farmer shot a wild cat which he suspected of damaging his hens, and threw it to an African whose totem he knew it to be, saying 'OK, how about eating that?' The name Mau-Mau is a reference to this cat.)[9]

Thus I suggest that theorists who have hoped to find a clear, unmistakable definition of 'the human community' simply given as part of the natural history of our species are likely to be disappointed. They will no doubt find it irritating to be asked to pay attention, at the outset of this topic, to a set of customs which they probably regard as confused, primitive, superstitious and objectionable. But if the argument used here is really to be an empirical one, then the range of existing and reported customs is the proper evidence for it. It might have been true that people always and everywhere showed an unfailing regard for their species-barrier, that they naturally always accepted any member of their own species into fellowship without difficulty, and were never even tempted to form bonds with members of other species. We might have found too that they were always quite clear about their ancestral tree, and included in it no being who was not manifestly *sapiens*. We do not find this. Besides totemism, we find many links with particular species, such as that of the Masai with their cattle, and of nomads with their horses, which, while rather more Utilitarian, play so important a part in social life that the community cannot be properly thought of without them. Tractors cannot be substituted. (Wherever there are horses, there are some people who actually prefer them to humans. This attitude is generally frowned upon, but it persists all the same.) Man does not naturally exist in species-isolation.

13 NATURE SUPPLIES NO PLAIN LINE

What should we conclude from all this? Obviously, we have no reason to conclude that existing views on this subject ought always to be accepted. On the issue of undue exclusion, no doubt we shall all agree that they ought not. Advancing morality has everywhere steadily worked to flatten out that side of the discrepancy, to insist that even foreigners are humans, and ought in principle to be treated as brothers. I think that there is in the West, though not in Buddhism, quite a widespread impression that flattening out the other side as well –

excluding all non-humans to whom some sympathy and status have been extended – is merely a necessary part of this same enterprise, and ought obviously to be combined with it. This idea sometimes takes the form of assuming that the mere curtailing of sympathy and attention given to animals will, automatically, and as it were hydraulically, make more energy available for helping humans, rather as pushing in one bulge on a damaged can may straighten out another. This is not obvious. It would be so only if, as we suggested in Chapter 2, our duties could be represented by a series of concentric circles, each containing claims closer and more urgent than the one outside it, and if the species-barrier were clearly a circle right outside all those involving humans. But as we saw there, this set of concentric circles cannot be consistently drawn up at all. Claims are of different kinds. Those on behalf of one's own community certainly are strong, but they are not the only strong kind. And the species-barrier, as we now find, is not even accepted in the same form by all human communities. But also, more important than this, all these communities are themselves multi-species ones. It is one of the special powers and graces of our species not to ignore others, but to draw in, domesticate and live with a great variety of other creatures. No other animal does so on anything like so large a scale. Perhaps we should take this peculiar human talent more seriously and try to understand its workings. We will turn to this in the next chapter.

10 The Mixed Community

I THE WELL-FILLED STAGE

All human communities have involved animals. Those present in them always include, for a start, some dogs, with whom our association seems to be an incredibly ancient one, amounting to symbiosis. But besides them an enormous variety of other creatures, ranging from reindeer to weasels and from elephants to shags, has for ages also been domesticated. Of course they were largely there for use – for draught and riding, for meat, milk, wool and hides, for feathers and eggs, as vermin-catchers or as aids to fishing and hunting. In principle, it might seem reasonable to expect that these forms of exploitation would have produced no personal or emotional involvement at all. From a position of ignorance, we might have expected that people would view their animals simply as machines. If we impose the sharp Kantian dichotomy between *persons* and *things*, subjects and objects, and insist that everything must be considered as simply one or the other, we might have expected that they would be viewed unambiguously as things. But in fact, if people had viewed them like this, the domestication could probably never have worked. The animals, with the best will in the world, could not have reacted like machines. They became tame, not just through the fear of violence, but because they were able to form individual bonds with those who tamed them by coming to understand the social signals addressed to them. They learned to obey human beings personally. They were able to do this, not only because the people taming them were social beings, but because they themselves were so as well.

All creatures which have been successfully domesticated are ones which were originally social. They have transferred to human beings the trust and docility which, in a wild state, they would have developed towards their parents, and in adult life towards the leaders of their pack or herd. There are other, and perhaps equally intelligent, creatures which it is quite impossible to tame, because they simply do not have the innate capacity to respond to social signals in their own species, and therefore cannot reach those which come from outside. The various kinds of wild cat are an impressive example. Even their youngest kittens are quite untamable. Egyptian cats, from which all our domestic moggies are descended, are unique among the small-cat group in their sociability. It is interesting that they do not seem to have been domesticated in Egypt before about 1600 BC, and after that time they quickly became extremely popular.[1] Unless they were only discovered then – which would be odd – it seems that there may have been an actual mutation at that point producing a more responsive constitution.

Cats, however, are notoriously still not sociable or docile in quite the same way as dogs. Circus people do not usually waste their time trying to train cats. Similarly, there are important differences between the social natures, as well as the physiques, of horses, mules, donkeys, camels and the like. Both as species and as individuals they react variously to training; they cannot be treated just as standard-issue physical machines. People who succeed well with them do not do so just by some abstract, magical human superiority, but by interacting socially with them – by attending to them and coming to understand how various things appear from each animal's point of view. To ignore or disbelieve in the existence of that point of view would be fatal to the attempt. The traditional assumption behind the domestication of animals has been that, as Thomas Nagel has put it, there is something which it is to be a bat,[2] and similarly there is something which it is to be a horse or donkey, and to be *this* horse or donkey. There is not, by contrast, any such experience as *being* a stone, or a model-T Ford, or even a jet-plane. There is no being which could have that experience, so mechanics do not have to attend to it.

2 EXPLOITATION REQUIRES SYMPATHY

I am saying that this has been the traditional assumption. Modern Behaviourists who think it a false one can of course argue against it. My present point is simply that their opinion is a recent and sophisticated one. It is not the view which has been taken for granted during the long centuries in which animals have been domesticated. If we ask an Indian farmer whether he supposes that the ox which he is beating can feel, he is likely to answer, 'Certainly it can, otherwise why would I bother?' A skilled horseman needs to respond to his horse as an individual, to follow the workings of its feelings, to use his imagination in understanding how things are likely to affect it, what frightens it and what attracts it, as much as someone who wants to control human beings needs to do the same thing. Horses and dogs are addressed by name, and are expected to understand what is said to them. Nobody tries this with stones or hammers or jet-planes. The treatment of domestic animals has never been impersonal. We can say that they are not 'persons', because (apart from the Trinity) that word does generally signify *Homo sapiens*. But they are certainly not viewed just as things. They are animals, a category which, for purposes of having a point of view belongs, not with things, but with people.

This point is important because it shows what may seem rather surprising – a direct capacity in man for attending to, and to some extent understanding, the moods and reactions of other species. No doubt this capacity is limited. Human callousness makes some of its limitations obvious. But then, similar callousness is also often found in our dealings with other human beings. The question whether somebody knows what suffering he is causing may be a hard one to answer in either case. The callous person may not positively *know*, because he does not want to; he does not attend. But he could know if he chose to scan the evidence. This seems to be equally true in either case. The reason for overworking an ox or horse is usually much the same as that for overworking a human slave – not that one does not believe that they mind it, or supposes that they cannot even notice it, but that one is putting one's own interest first. The treatment of domestic animals resembles that of slaves in being extremely patchy and variable. There is not normally a steady, unvarying disregard, such as should follow if one genuinely supposed that the creature was not sentient at all, or if one was quite unable to guess what its feelings might be. Disregard is varied by partial spasmodic kindness, and also by spasmodic cruelty. And cruelty is something which could have no point for a person who really did not believe the victim to have definite feelings. (There is very little comfort in working off ill-temper on a cushion.) Family pigs are often treated with real pride and affection during their lives, they may even be genuinely mourned – only this will not protect them from being eaten. Horses, bell-wethers, Lapp reindeer and the cattle of the Masai can similarly receive real regard, can be treated as dear companions and personally cherished, can form part of human households in a different way from any machine or inanimate treasure[3] – only they will still on suitable occasions be killed or otherwise ill-treated if human purposes demand it. But we should notice too a similar arbitrariness often appearing in the treatment of human dependants, so that we can scarcely argue that there is no real capacity for sympathy towards the animals. In the treatment of other people, of course, our natural caprice is constantly disciplined by the deliberate interference of morality. We know that we must not eat our grandmothers or our children merely because they annoy us. Over animals this restraint is usually much less active; caprice has much freer play. That does not mean that they are taken not to be conscious. Belief in their sentience is essential even for exploiting them successfully.

3 THE IMPLAUSIBILITY OF SCEPTICISM

This point matters because it tells strongly against the Behaviourist idea that the subjective feelings of animals are all, equally, quite hidden from us, cannot concern us and may well not even exist. This idea is often expressed by saying that belief in them is illicitly *anthropomorphic*. The notion of anthropomorphism is a very interesting one; we must look at it shortly. But straight away I want to point out how odd it would be if those who, over many centuries, have depended on working with animals, turned out to have been relying on a sentimental and pointless error in doing so, an error which could be corrected at a stroke by metaphysicians who may never have encountered those animals at all. For instance – working elephants can still only be successfully handled by mahouts who live in close and life-long one-to-one relations with them. Each mahout treats his elephant, not like a tractor, but like a basically benevolent if often tiresome uncle, whose moods must be understood and handled very much like those of a human colleague. If there were any less expensive and time-consuming way of getting work out of elephants, the Sri Lankan timber trade would by now certainly have discovered it. Obviously the mahouts may have many beliefs about the elephants which are false because they are 'anthropomorphic' – that is, they misinterpret some outlying aspects of elephant behaviour by relying on a human pattern which is inappropriate. But if they were doing this about the basic everyday feelings – about whether their elephant is pleased, annoyed, frightened, excited, tired, sore, suspicious or angry – they would not only be out of business, they would often simply be dead. And to describe and understand such moods, they use the same general vocabulary which is used for describing humans.

Nearer home, here is an example from the memoirs of a blind woman being taught to walk with a guide-dog. The dog-trainer says,

> 'Don't stop talking, or Emma'll think you've fallen asleep . . . You've got to keep her interest. She's a dog, and there are lots of nice, interesting smells all round, and things passing which you can't see. So unless you talk to her, she'll get distracted, and stop to sniff a lamp-post.'[4]

This is a particularly good example, because it makes so clear the point that there is no question of illicitly attributing human sensibility. The trainer – whose interest is of course purely practical – is at pains to point out just what is distinctive about the dog's own sensibilities, simply because they must be allowed for if it is to do its work. But to make this point, he necessarily and properly uses the same words (interest, distract, she'll think you've fallen asleep) which would be used in a comparable human case. The wide difference between the two species does not affect the correctness of this language at all.

This is not, of course, the only context where a Behaviourist approach runs into difficulties. It encounters grave problems about the possibility of attributing subjective feelings to other humans, as well as to animals. I do not think that this problem will turn out very different for animals, certainly not in cases where either the feeling is very strong or the species is very familiar. The charge of 'anthropomorphism' as a general objection to attributing *any* feelings to animals, rather than to attributing the wrong feelings, is probably a red herring.

4 WHAT ARE PETS?

Before we come to this larger point, however, we need to go into an aspect of the matter which might seem still more remarkable and unexpected to an observer who was totally ignorant of human affairs. This is the real individual affection, rather than exploitation, which can arise between animals and people. Since pet-keeping is sometimes denounced as a gratuitous perversion produced by modern affluence, I take a respectably ancient example from the prophet Nathan:

> The poor man had nothing save one little ewe lamb, which he had bought and nourished up; and it grew up together with him, and with his children; it did eat of his own morsel, and drank of his own cup, and lay in his bosom, and was to him as a daughter.[5]

Several things should be noticed here.

1. The man is *poor*. We are not dealing with the follies of the idle rich.

2. He is not childless; his children share the lamb's company with him.

3. The relation is regarded as a perfectly natural one.

Nathan chooses this story confidently to enlist King David's sympathy for the lamb-keeper. When he goes on to tell how the rich man killed this lamb for a feast, David breaks out in horror, 'As the Lord liveth, the man that has done this is worthy to die.' This makes it possible for Nathan to say 'Thou art the man!' and to apply the fable to David's treatment of Uriah the Hittite. But what would Nathan have said if David had replied that of course poor men can expect that sort of thing to happen if they will go in for sentimental pet-keeping instead of adopting human orphans? Clearly no such answer was on the cards. David knows as well as Nathan does what the lamb meant to the poor man, and both understand clearly how this strong individual relation was possible, even in a society where lambs were being killed all the time. This paradoxical ambivalence of pastoral and hunting peoples comes out very often in the metaphors of Christ. The good shepherd lays down his life for his sheep, he searches out every single lost sheep and cherishes it – yet the Passover Lamb is eaten at the last supper, and in general this must be the destiny of nearly all Hebrew sheep. It is, to an economic eye, the main reason why they are kept at all.

5 THE FLEXIBILITY OF PARENT–CHILD BEHAVIOUR

It is hopeless trying to understand this situation if we keep pressing the crude Kantian question, 'but are lambs people or things?' If we want to grasp it, we must wake up to a much wider range of possibilities. Our conceptual map needs revising. In extending it, our first guiding light should be the thought that the poor man's lamb 'was to him as a daughter'. His love for it was the kind of love suited to a child. He loved it in this way, *not* because he had no children and was so undiscriminating that he was ready to deceive himself and cuddle a cushion, but because the lamb really was a live creature needing love, and it was able to respond to parental cherishing. This is not fetishism, but a perfectly normal feeling. The appeal of small and helpless creatures is not limited by species. Animals in the wild certainly do not normally notice young outside their own kind, but if they are thrown together with them, as they are in captivity, they often respond in a remarkable way: they can adopt. Full-scale adoption is sometimes possible, even in the wild.[6] And it is striking how domestic animals will put up with rough treatment from small children, which they would certainly not tolerate from adults. How, we ask, does the cat know that a baby much larger than itself is a child – is, in effect, a kitten? What the signals are does not matter much – some of them may well be chemical. But if we ourselves were presented with a baby elephant, and had a chance to watch and take in its playful behaviour, we would be able to grasp the same point.

Play-signals penetrate species-barriers with perfect ease.[7] What is even more interesting is the startling set of emotional and practical consequences which the adult animal draws from the signals. The cat shows a mood of tolerance, playfulness and positive affection which would astonish us if we did not ourselves so readily share it. Of course it would be no use trying this kind of appeal on a codfish. Infantile signals work only with species which cherish their own young. And even there, the gap must not be too large if the message is to get across. Birds would in general be unlikely to decipher human infantile signals; if the ravens fed Elijah, it seems that he must have gaped like a young cuckoo. But where the message does get across, its power in producing fellowship is astonishing. It affects not only adults, but other young as well, releasing in them the hope of play. The human baby makes a bee-line for the cat. The cat, if it is a kitten, returns the compliment with particular fervour. Both are inquisitive and playful. This attraction seems, again, to be common to all those relatively intelligent species which are capable of play. In wild conditions, it normally will not overcome the stronger tendency to species-imprinting unless playmates of one's own species are uncommonly scarce, as in the case which Jane Goodall describes. But in a mixed human community it can very well do so. None of the creatures present is getting a really exclusive imprinting. Accordingly, the species-barrier there, imposing though it may look, is rather like one of those tall wire fences whose impressiveness is confined to their upper reaches. To an adult in formal dress, engaged on his official statesmanly interactions, the fence is an insuperable barrier. Down below, where it is full of holes, it presents no obstacle at all. The young of *Homo sapiens*, like those of the other species present, scurry through it all the time. Since all human beings start life as children, this has the quite important consequence that hardly any of us, at heart, sees the social world as an exclusively human one.

6   THE CHILD'S QUEST FOR VARIETY

To spell this out: The point is not just that most human beings have in fact been acquainted with other creatures early in life, and have therefore received some non-human imprinting. It is also that children who are not offered this experience often actively seek it. Animals, like song and dance, are an innate taste. Even those whose homes have contained none often seek them out and find them irresistible. The fact seems too obvious to need mentioning and does not usually attract much criticism. Even people who believe that there is something perverse and wrong about adults taking an interest in animals are often quite content that children should do so. Like some other interests which appeal to children it may, however, be considered as something which one ought to grow out of. Prolonged interest in it may seem a sign of emotional immaturity. Behind this thought lies the more general idea that animals are suitable only as practice material for the immature, because they are in effect nothing but simplified models of human beings. On this pattern, those who graduate past them to real human relationships are not expected to have any further interest in them, any more than a real golfer does in clock-golf in the park.

This way of thinking has a certain point, but beyond the crudest level it can be very misleading. No animal is just a simplified human being, nor do children take them to be so. However friendly they may be, their life is radically foreign, and it is just that foreignness which attracts a child. The point about them is that they are different. As for immaturity, it is of course true that we must all come to terms first and foremost with our own species. Those unwilling to do this can indeed seek refuge with animals, as they can in other activities. But the mere fact of taking an interest in animals does not show that kind of motive, any more than taking an interest in machines or music does. Experience of animals is not essentially a substitute for experience of people, but a supplement to it – something more which is needed for a full human life. The ewe lamb did not come between the poor man and his children. Instead it formed an extra delight which he could share with them, and so strengthened the family bond. (That, surely, is why Nathan mentions the children.) One sort of love does not need to block another, because love, like compassion, is not a rare fluid to be economized, but a capacity which grows by use. And if we ask (again impersonating an ignorant observer) whether the limits of its natural use in human beings coincide with the species-barrier, we see plainly that they do not. In early childhood that barrier scarcely operates. And even in later life it seldom becomes absolute.

7   NEOTENY AND EXTENDED SYMPATHY

There are two likely reasons for this extra emotional porousness of the human species-barrier. The less interesting one is sheer security. Animal mothers are often nervous of letting their children play with outsiders, and this is not foolish; real dangers often do threaten. (Chimps, for instance, do occasionally eat baby baboons.) Human life by contrast is usually secure enough to allow some wider experiment. But the second and more profound reason is simply the much greater intensity of human sympathy and curiosity. That eager reaching-out to surrounding life and to every striking aspect of the physical world, which in other species belongs only to infancy, persists in human beings much longer, and may be present throughout their lives. Humans are *neotenous* – that is, they prolong certain infantile characteristics into maturity, develop them and continue to profit by them as adults. From an evolutionary point of view, this may be the main key to their exceptional development. People retain as adults a number of physical marks which in other primates are found only in infants or in embryos, the most notable of which is, of course, the great size and long-continued growth of the brain. They also retain some marked infantile patterns of behaviour, among which is a tendency to play of all sorts, including such things as imitating, singing, dancing and the making of objects for pleasure, habits on which the arts are based. Adults among other advanced species do indeed sometimes play together, and their doing so is rightly seen as a sign of intelligence. But they all do it far less than humans.[8] The real corner-stones of these prolonged and intensified infantile faculties, however, probably do not lie in play itself, but in the sympathy and curiosity which underly it. Man at his best is no longer satisfied to confine these two motives within the grooves of habit. He continually reaches out to further use of them. But this insatiability of interest is itself characteristic of childhood. Of course when it is extended into adult life it takes on a different meaning. But it is a faculty retained and put to use, not a faculty invented.

Neoteny raises the whole question of 'childishness' – of what can, and what cannot, rightly be kept and used from early life by an individual moving into maturity. To St Paul, this question looked very easy. As he said, 'When I was a child, I spoke as a child, I thought as a child, I understood as a child; but when I became a man, I put aside childish things.'[9] This position looks sensible. The trouble about it is that those who take it have often included among the 'childish things' on the rubbish-pile matters absolutely central to life. They have, indeed, sometimes lost all interest in life itself because they have parted with aspects of it without which it ceases to be worth living. Erik Berne suggests a deeper view – that the child in each of us is never lost, but remains active at the core of our being:

> The Child is in many ways the most valuable part of the personality, and can contribute to the individual's life exactly what an actual child can contribute to family life; charm, pleasure and creativity. If the Child in the individual is confused and unhealthy, then the consequences may be unfortunate, but something can and should be done about it.[10]

The capacity for widely extended sympathy, for social horizons not limited to one's familiar group, is certainly a part of this childish spontaneity. It is also the window through which interest in creatures of other species enters our lives, both in childhood and – if we do not firmly close the window – in later life as well. It is one aspect of that openness to new impressions, that relative freedom from constraining innate programmes, which makes us culturally malleable and enables us, through pseudo-speciation, to accept and build such varied ways of life. It carries with it, too, that still wider curiosity, that capacity for interest in other, inanimate surrounding objects – plants and stones, stars, rocks and water – which extends our horizon beyond the social into the ecological, and makes us true citizens of the world. In theory we might, perhaps, have been creatures who enjoyed none of this liberty, who were programmed from birth to be capable only of interesting ourselves in the doings of our own species. But Fate has not been so mean.

A rather touching example of this wider power of human sympathy occurs when Jane Goodall describes the effect of a polio epidemic on the chimpanzees she was studying. One old animal, his legs wholly paralysed by the disease, was dragging himself around with his arms. He was suffering from loneliness, since he, like the other crippled individuals, was shunned and sometimes attacked by those who were still healthy. In the hope of inducing two companions who were grooming each other to groom him as well, he dragged himself up into a tree:

> With a loud grunt of pleasure he reached a hand towards them in greeting – but even before he made contact they both swung quickly away and, without a backward glance, started grooming on the far side of the tree. For a full two minutes, old Gregor sat motionless, staring after them. And then he laboriously lowered himself to the ground. As I watched him sitting there alone, my vision blurred, and when I looked up at the groomers in the tree *I came nearer to hating a chimpanzee than I have ever done before or since.*[11]

As she well knows, it would be unfair to hate them, since they are incapable of reacting otherwise. Their response is one which of course is perfectly possible for humans also, and indeed is often found among them. They are repelled by the damaged individual, and really do not see him as their old friend at all, but as something strange and alarming. Chimpanzees can only occasionally break through this barrier and cherish a sick comrade – wolves, elephants, dolphins and whales are known to do it rather more often. People, however, have, if they care to use it, a much wider capacity still, one which is perfectly able to function like this right across the species-barrier. Jane Goodall and her colleagues do not only get upset about Gregor's situation, they do everything they can to relieve it.

8 EVOLUTIONARY CONSIDERATIONS

Is this wider power of sympathy at all surprising, or is it what one would naturally expect for a species in our position? So far I have treated this as an open question, and said that 'in theory' – that is before investigation – an intelligent species might, for all we know, really be isolated emotionally from all surrounding species, might view them simply as moving objects and have no access to their moods. But this 'theoretical' isolated possibility is actually very obscure and may perhaps not make much sense. Biological questions often cannot be asked in isolation like this. To ask 'could there be an intelligent species with no senses?' or 'living in total solitude?' is scarcely comprehensible. If we say 'no' to these ideas, we are not ruling about the possibilities of forms of life totally unknown to us, but clarifying the meaning which concepts like 'intelligence' can have to us here and now. The difficulty about imagining a species cut off in this way from all its neighbours is in the first place a practical one. Apart from deliberate communication at close quarters (which is all we have mentioned so far) species make use of all kinds of unintended signals from each other, and to interpret these they need to grasp the moods that underly them. For hunting, and also for avoiding danger from predators and other threatening creatures, it is vitally necessary to recognize fear, anger, suspicion, territorial outrage and a dozen other moods. Warnings and hints can also be gained all the time from the conduct of creatures which are not interested in oneself at all. But it needs interpretation. This is the sort of thing in which people living in the wilds often excel, and they need to do so. What looks to the urban oik like a mere silly mob of excited birds means to the instructed local perhaps an indication of approaching predators – perhaps food available in the neighbourhood, perhaps a sign of approaching migration, and therefore an unexpectedly early winter, perhaps a score of further important things which the townsman would never think of.

The local is able to interpret these, partly of course by sheer experience, but also (as we shall shortly see) probably because human neurological processes have not diverged far enough from those of the birds to make sympathetic interpretation impossible or even difficult. To get rid of that similarity, physical changes would be needed, and they would apparently be disadvantageous.

Evolutionarily speaking, then, it is likely that a species such as ours would find itself equipped for the position which some Old Testament texts give it,[12] of steward and guardian, under God, placed over a range of creatures which he is in principle able to care for and understand, rather than in the one often imagined in science fiction, of an invader exploiting an entirely alien planet.

Many of those who are anxious to distract human attention from animals would not, of course, want to deny that this is true; they would simply say that it is a pity.

9 THE STIGMA OF SAVAGERY

Critics who object to attempts at inter-species communication often do not take the theoretical Behaviourist line that these attempts are simply impossible. They do not doubt the success, but the desirability of the enterprise. They see themselves as standing for an adult, civilized attitude against goings-on which are primitive and childish. They recommend indifference to animals – and indeed to all non-human nature – as a condition of emotional maturity. Ought this advice to impress us? It is not obvious why it should. Emotional maturity is not necessarily achieved by limiting one's emotional commitments, nor by rejecting interests held in common with children. Increasing callousness is, on the whole, rather a bad sign for it. Children and 'primitives' need not always be wrong.

The view that an adult and civilized approach cannot fail to remove such interests is remarkably well expressed in the article on 'Animals' in that magisterial work, the *Encyclopaedia of Religion and Ethics*.

Writing in 1908, before certain embarrassments descended on the human end of the argument, the author explains:

> Civilization, or perhaps rather education, has brought with it a sense of the great gulf that exists between man and the lower animals . . . In the lower stages of culture, whether they be found in races which are, as a whole, below the European level, or in the uncultured portion of civilized communities, the distinction between men and animals is not adequately, if at all, recognized . . . The savage . . . attributes to the animal a vastly more complex set of thoughts and feelings, and a much greater range of knowledge and power, than it actually possesses . . . It is therefore small wonder that his attitude towards the animal creation is one of reverence rather than superiority.

The author does not bring, as support for his more enlightened views, any evidence of a zoological kind to show that those who were familiar with the animals actually knew less about their capacities than those who were not. The locals have, of course, often been found to be mistaken, on particular points, but they can only be shown to be so by empirical inquiry. In fact, ethological investigation, once it was vigorously set on foot in this century, has shown that Western urban thought was (not surprisingly) often even more ill-informed than local superstition on many such questions, and that it had consistently attributed to animals a vastly *less* complex set of thoughts and feelings, and a much smaller range of knowledge and power, than they actually possessed. The only fact to which the author appeals is that animals do not talk. This is true, but he does not explain why language should be the only quality to deserve respect. He does, however, considerately account for the errors of the heathen, as follows:

> One of the main sources of the respect paid to animals is the belief that certain species are the embodiments of the souls of the dead . . . Thus a kind of alliance springs up between certain human kins and certain species of animals, in which some writers have sought the germ of totemism.

In this way respect for animals is accounted for as a by-product of a false belief in reincarnation. That explanation seems to put the cart (or coffin) before the horse. Belief in reincarnation must surely be seen as an expression, or consequence, of a previous high opinion of those animals. In fact, apart from the point about speech, the grounds for correcting primitive views here scarcely seem to be factual at all.

They are moral, but they do not get the support of explicit moral argument. The reference to 'civilization, or perhaps rather education' as making this desirable change does not seem to be an appeal to any special scientific knowledge of animals, but rather to the general rationalistic European tradition which we have discussed earlier. From this point of view, the criticism made against both primitives and children is not that they are *ignorant* – that they credit animals with feelings which they actually do not have – but that they are frivolous, are occupying themselves with something unimportant.

In this chapter, we have looked at the natural, emotional preference for one's own species over others which seems to underlie much conduct attacked as 'speciesist', and have found reason to admit its existence and to treat it with considerable respect, but no reason to think it an impenetrable social barrier, cutting us off from other creatures in a way which makes them none of our proper concern. On the factual question whether, and how much, humans are naturally equipped to notice and respond to the moods of other species, we find that their equipment is quite good, rather better than that of other comparable creatures, though all have some gifts that way.

This has some rather interesting consequences. We have to consider next the sceptical position that the use of ordinary social and emotional language to refer to animals is illegitimate because it is 'anthropomorphic'. This attack assumes that human language is invented in the first place not only *by* humans, but exclusively *about* humans – to describe them and them alone. Any use of it to describe any other being would then be an 'extension' – a leap out into the unknown. But if language has, from the start, arisen in a mixed community and has been adapted to describe all beings whose moods etc. might be of general importance and interest, then that is the proper use of the concepts from the start, and no leap is needed. We will look at this problem, and at others surrounding the notion of anthropomorphism, in the next chapter.

11 *What is Anthropomorphism?*

I GODS AND BEASTS

Anthropomorphism is a remarkable concept. It may be the only example of a notion invented solely for God, and then transferred unchanged to refer to animals. The word itself is old. The 'anthropomorphite heresy' was that of certain very early Christians who believed God actually to have a human shape or 'morph'. Their error, of course, was not supposed to lie in giving him the wrong shape (as if he had really been a star) but in giving him any physical shape at all. This sense was the only one the word had until about a century ago, when it was somewhat suddenly extended to cover the attribution of some human qualities to non-human animals. Thus the O E D, after mentioning God, gives the general meaning of 'anthropomorphic' as 'attributing a human personality to *anything impersonal or irrational*' and defines an anthropomorphist as 'one who uses anthropomorphism, or attributes a human personality to *God, abstract ideas, other animals, etc.*' (my italics). What class does that *etc.* cover? What is the common bond welding the impersonal to the irrational and linking the three examples given? It seems to be merely their not being human. But the ways in which a given thing differs from the various things which it is *not* are themselves various. Buttered toast does not differ from the Tower Bridge in the same way in which it differs from the square root of π, and mistaking it for the first will produce different confusions from mistaking it for the second. The dictionary's strange list of contrasts lights up a difficulty which continually blocks very large-scale discussions of mankind. There are not very many kinds of being with whom mankind can usefully be compared and contrasted, and those few that there are are rather mixed. The most familiar of them are (1) God and (2) other animals. The only other obvious candidate is the class of machines. As for abstract ideas, no doubt they can be classed with God for some purposes, but mostly for negative ones. Ideas do not obviously need to be treated as existing objects at all. 'Personifying' rather than 'anthropomorphizing' is the word commonly used to describe those who represent them as existing in the form of people. This seems sensible, because the idea of

125

'personifying' is one about existence. And existence is not the point in the other three cases. Someone who complains of anthropomorphic views about God is not expressing doubts about whether he exists, but about whether he is being rightly conceived. Similarly those who complain of animals and machines being viewed anthropomorphically are not protesting that they really do not exist. They are complaining about the particular qualities attributed to them. It is not obvious that these complaints are at all of the same kind over God as they are over the other two cases. It will be best to consider God's case first.

What then is the *morph* or shape with which, as more subtle believers have held, God ought not to be credited? It is of course not only the literal, physical form. There are many human qualities of mind as well as of body – needs, weaknesses, confusions, defects and limitations of all kinds – which it becomes unsuitable to attribute to a god, as soon as your idea of him becomes rather more exalted.

2   DISSOLVING GOD

The Greeks early saw the need for this kind of criticism of the rampantly human gods portrayed by Homer. Xenophanes, in the sixth century BC, dropped one of the most penetrating remarks ever made on the topic when he said that, if an ox could paint, his god would look like an ox, and used this thought to discredit the myths altogether. But Xenophanes was not an atheist. He still believed in a god 'who is not like men in appearance or in mind'.[1] Any reverent person can easily start this reform, but it has proved very hard to know how far to take it. The words *or in mind* can carry us very far. The solvent which clears God of vices tends strongly also to wipe out his virtues. If a being never feels fear, can he be brave? If he never feels desire, can he be temperate? If he knows everything already, can he be wise? More generally, how can a being without need or weakness of any kind, and without position in time or space, have any aims or be concerned about anything or anyone? Mainstream Christianity and Judaism stop fairly soon on this road, retaining a 'personal' God who, in spite of his eternity and omnipotence, is really concerned as a father for his creatures, loves them individually and is deeply involved in the processes of history. If you have a god at all, this is not obviously wrong, so the term 'personality' may not be inappropriate. But there is also in Christianity a quite strong continuing strand of 'negative theology' which resists all such ideas as inadequate metaphors and is unwilling to call God anything, even good. It repeats for every attribution the disclaimer 'whatever we say, Thou art not that'. This way of thinking can remain religious, as it does even in its much more advanced reaches in

Buddhism. But of course it can also be used in a much more drastic and literal way to get rid, not only of the idea of God, but of religious thinking altogether.

3   THE SCEPTICAL ARGUMENT

The difference between these two conclusions, important though it is, does not concern us now. What we now need to worry about is the earlier, sceptical stage of the reasoning, the argument which apparently runs:

Our idea of *x* (in this case God) is made up of elements drawn from human life:

But *x* is not human:

Therefore that idea is only a mirror and tells us nothing about *x*.

Now this argument is not really impressive because it proves far too much. It suggests that the sphere of 'human life' can never be extended. Yet it often is extended. Every new thing that we meet has to be understood in terms drawn from earlier human experience. This is inevitable, because 'understanding' anything new simply *is* relating it to what we have already experienced, finding a way to bring it within reach of our existing range of concepts. The newness of the new thing has to be assimilated or digested in this way if we are to make it ours. Of course sceptics are right to point out that we make all kinds of mistakes in doing this. But this argument cannot support a more drastic scepticism, because the mistakes can only count as mistakes if we take the correcting insight to be less mistaken.

Sceptics are also right to remind us that we can never comprehend anything completely. Even those who have got used to electric light, and have (as we say) a real scientific grasp of how it works, still have not incorporated its full detail and meaning into their thought. Nor has even its inventor done so. What we know must always be taken as a mere flea-bite on what we do not know. We are not equipped to swallow the universe. But then fortunately this is not what is needed. Specialists in the physics of electric light have an adequate working notion, which is certainly not just a mirror of their own former experience. Most, perhaps nearly all, of its elements are drawn from that experience. But they are re-arranged in a way which is quite new, and which does reflect and depend on the new phenomenon outside. Electricity is not just a projection of our private images and desires. And to move to an instance nearer to our present purpose: Within human life, someone who makes a friend from an age-group or culture unlike his own will have no choice but to use materials from his own previous experience as a guide to understanding him. As the friendship grows, he will repeatedly see the mistakes which he has made by doing this badly. But he certainly would not do better by waiting for some miracle which would make him a member of the unknown culture right away. By persisting, he partly corrects his mistakes, and in doing this he does not move to some sterilized range of experience which is not his own. He uses his own experience more instructedly and intelligently and adds to it. The proper notion of 'understanding' cannot be one which prevents anything new from ever being understood at all.

4 UNREAL ISOLATION

These very general remarks are meant to shed doubt on a certain dogmatic and unrealistic sceptical isolation of human life from every possible context, which has made many sorts of communication look unintelligible, in spite of the fact that they work. The case of God is complicated by problems about his existence, and I cannot say much about it now. As with animals, and indeed with electricity, it is of course quite sensible to ask whether he was really outside the human sphere in the first place. My present point is, however, just that he cannot be shown to be totally unknowable, or not to exist, simply because our ideas of him are made up of human elements and expressed in human terms. All our ideas are so. The objection to 'anthropomorphism' over our ideas of God, though useful enough in its most obvious applications, very quickly lets us down when we try to make it confront more difficult problems. At first the 'morph', the quality we are objecting to, is something obviously wrong in itself – physical shape and size, folly, weakness, vice. But next comes the question 'is emotion as a whole, or even thinking as we understand it, part of this objectionable human morph? Does that include every aspect of human personality?' The argument which I have just criticized says that it must do so, simply because personality, emotion and so forth are human. But this means ruling that God – and indeed all non-human life – must be so unlike us that none of it can be understood from a human standpoint at all. This seems to be an arbitrary, groundless dogma. In the case of animals, evolution makes it most implausible.

I think that in fact the word 'anthropomorphism' is not only clumsy but really misleading as soon as we get away from its literal application to shape or form. It is in principle an open question whether any given particular quality can belong either to God (granted that he exists) or to animals. These questions cannot be answered simply by noting that that quality does belong to people. The real and serious fault of groundlessly attributing unsuitable human qualities to these beings from mere force of habit is better described as undue *humanizing* ('*Representing as human*' OED). This already respectable word needs to be supplemented by an explanation of just what is undue on a particular occasion. It is not an automatic term of abuse. It does not carry the strange suggestion that we already know just what the whole human 'morph' is, and have established that none of it is to be found elsewhere. Just how misleading this suggestion can be when we come to animals we shall now see from a couple of examples. They are both from the OED, which gives these two citations from a book called *Seaside Studies* by G. H. Lewes, published in 1858. They treat the matter very much as it is still constantly treated. They run thus:

1. We speak with large latitude of anthropomorphism when we speak of the 'vision' of these animals (molluscs).

2. As we are just now looking with scientific seriousness at our animals, we will discard all anthropomorphic interpretations, such as point to 'alarm'.

This is surely strange talk. The charge here cannot be that of 'attributing a human personality' because the things attributed have no bearing on personality: they are common aspects of animal life. 'Vision' here does not refer to some special kind of spiritual vision; it simply means 'sight'. But sight is a faculty which people have as animals, which they share with other animals and indeed which they presumably would not have if they were bodiless minds. Both the optics and the physiology of it are matters for physical scientists, who are in principle equally interested in its working across the whole range of species, and would think it superstitious and objectionable to suggest that the whole meaning of 'sight' became changed at the human species-frontier. What about 'alarm'? It is not obvious here, either, what there is in that term to bring a blush to the cheek of scientific seriousness. The physiology of fear, and its connection with such reactions as flight, hiding and inactivity, has been explored for the human species as for others, and very close likenesses have been found, along with the usual range of equally interesting variations. Physiologists do not throw up their hands when they reach the human case and demand a quite new set of concepts. Nor do zoologists, when observing the behaviour of frightened birds or fish, find that everyday descriptions like 'alarm' suddenly lose their application, or lead to wrong predictions, and that a new set of terms needs to be invented. Embarrassment about the use of such words is not scientific. It is metaphysical. The words arouse suspicion, not because they are useless, but because of a philosophical view about what they might commit us to. And that view is mistaken.

5   EXAGGERATING THE PROBLEMS OF SUBJECTIVITY

The suspicion, of course, concerns inner experience. The critic is uneasy because he thinks that, if we say that a dog is alarmed or that it sees the river, we are claiming to know exactly how it feels. This would certainly be wild. But then it would also be wild in talking of human beings. Even where we know most clearly that another person is alarmed, or has seen the river, we can never share their experience. The barrier to sharing it is already a complete one with human beings, so it cannot be made any more complete by adding the species-barrier to it. We may suspect that the dog's experience would actually be more different from ours than another person's would. But that suspicion is irrelevant, since an impossibility cannot be made more impossible. Indeed it is not clear that any such comparison between unobservable differences makes any sense at all. The problem here is not about anthropomorphism, but about Behaviourism, and it arises already on the human scene. The barrier does not fall between us and the dog. It falls between you and me.

I can only deal briefly here with the answers to Behaviouristic scepticism. The essential point is that words like *sight* and *alarm*, *hunger, surprise* and even *pain*, are not the names of small private sensations at all, but refer to much larger slices of life and conduct, which include both public and private aspects. Behaviourists have been quite right to draw attention to the public aspect.[2] If alarm were *only* an internal feeling, which was never expressed in conduct, there could be no word for it. But, on the other side, the behaviour alone makes no sense without the inner element. In most cases, the only way to select and assemble the appropriate range of behaviour is to identify the right kind of experience first. Alarm can be expressed in an enormous variety of actions, including notably simply *not* doing things which nobody might have known one was otherwise inclined to do. No guiding thread would bring together that range for somebody who (like Wagner's Siegfried) had never felt fear himself, and so did not know the meaning of the word. Similarly, someone blind from birth would be at a great disadvantage in trying to investigate sight, however good the reports of it given to him might be. He could certainly get some grasp of it, partly by analogy with the senses which he did possess, and partly through the efforts of other people to translate their experience into his terms. But he would never have the concept of sight, nor those of light, colours etc., in the way that the rest of us do.

In the normal case – which of course is what the blind person has for the rest of his senses, and so for his general use of language – inner perception and observed conduct go together. Their correspondence, though rough, is good enough to give us our shared public world. We constantly check one against the other. We notice the reactions of others to our own way of acting and talking, and we interpret their actions by asking ourselves what our own feeling would be in their situation. We often do discover discrepancies – for instance about short sight or colour-blindness or what we find frightening. Moreover, because our expressive and sympathetic powers are well developed (for good evolutionary reasons which we will discuss shortly) we can often convey feelings to each other even though we cannot get inside each other's heads. Of course some cases are clearer than others. A moderate scepticism which points out that we are often over-confident, or indicates particular mistakes, is very welcome. But full-scale sceptical Behaviourism is not content with this; it insists that we can know *nothing* of each other's subjective experiences.

6 HOW WE SPOT EMOTIONS

This must extend to the clearest sort of case. Let us take that of someone in a towering and fully understandable rage – say, Macbeth at the point where he is desperately trying to find reassurance in the witches' prophecies, to persuade himself that he will not be crushed by the English army coming against him. The messenger sent to find out the size of that army creeps in, white and panic-stricken, unable to speak. At once Macbeth explodes, in fury:

> The devil damn thee black, thou cream-faced loon!
> Where got'st thou that goose look?

and goes on abusing him so uncontrollably that he can scarcely find a chance to deliver his message concerning the actual numbers. Now how plausible is it that Macbeth might, for all we know, at this time be in a state much like that of somebody else just dropping off to sleep, or setting out for a pleasant ride? Discussions of this topic are often distorted by being confined to a few marginal possibilities such as that he might be pretending. But if the scepticism is real, the whole range of conceivable moods ought to be equally likely. As for pretence, until we know the circumstances fully it is in principle a possibility. But in this case we do know them well enough to be sure that it would make no sense. Macbeth has no reason at all for wanting to make the servant think that he is angry; his anger will actually do harm. And pretence is in any case only possible as an occasional exception, against a background of normal cases where outer and inner states have their usual relation.

I have chosen this example because in it the anger is so irrational that it resists attempts to explain it in terms of conditioning or of behaviour calculated for a given end. It can in fact only be understood as the expression of a certain sort of subjective state – a state with which, in a general way, most of us are familiar, and which not only causes this sort of behaviour, but also explains it. In order to do this, it does not at all need to guarantee any close likeness between Macbeth's subjective feeling of anger and yours or mine. The generic likeness is sufficient. About likeness, the position can be compared with that where we want to buy an apple, but are assailed with sceptical doubts about whether it really is one or not, because the last apple which we ate is not available for a close comparison and matching of its taste with the new one. This predicament is not likely to bother us, because we know that what is required of apples is much more general and structural. And over feelings the same thing is true. We do not identify them, either in ourselves or other people, by directly matching a sensation, but by a wide variety of marks. Among these, sensations never stand alone. Someone may suspect that he himself is getting angry, in a way which is not unlike that in which he suspects that somebody else is. There are many possible warning indications. Fever is only one of them. In his own case, he does not settle this by some simple matching procedure comparable to consulting a colour-chart. He has not got his previous angry states before him, so this would scarcely be possible. Besides, mere fever might be physical.

To recognize states like anger is pattern-recognition. Such states involve characteristic shifts in the way in which a whole range of other subjective states relate to each other, and also to beliefs and tendencies to action. Commonly, they are marked most strongly by changes in the kinds of action which seem reasonable. Being angry is not just being slightly feverish; it is confronting a world in which other people look more hostile and threatening than they normally would. Actions of others which would normally appear harmless now seem like attacks upon one. The angry person is shorter than usual on confidence and serenity, and more inclined for aggression. He easily believes himself to be wronged. And so on. Now the extent of likeness which we can safely expect between the pattern of such reactions in ourselves and in others certainly depends on constitutional likeness as well as culture. In spite of some confusing cultural differences, it extends potentially throughout the species. Crusoe and Friday understand each other at once on some obvious points, and are in principle capable of coming to understand each other very well, because they are not just pieces of blank paper, variously inscribed by their different cultures, but conspecifics. Natural sympathy, as Hume rightly said, has a basis in common humanity. Does it therefore follow that it stops at the species-barrier?

7 UNDERSTANDING OTHER SPECIES

People have assumed so, and it seems to be what G. H. Lewes and those who have followed him have in mind. But it is not at all clear why anybody should assume it. The question seems to be an empirical one.

The fact that a power of understanding can be used on one's own species does not tend at all to show that it cannot work on others. It is an empirically established fact about human beings that they possess powers of expression and sympathy which make it possible for them to assess each other's subjective states, not in precise detail, but well enough to make an enormous difference to success in their understanding and treatment of each other. Where real care and attention are brought to bear, fine tuning of the common system can at times produce astonishing results. We ask next: does this work with other species? Do human beings, in their frequent interactions with other animals, manage to identify their moods and feelings too? This question can only be answered in terms of success, of improved interaction, resting on interpretation and prediction of their actions. But then that is true on the human scene as well. To go on using a concept successfully in a wide variety of situations *is* to have that concept. And the answer is that those who try to understand animals, and give time and attention to the matter, often come to understand them quite well. Those who do not, fail, which is also true with human beings.

12 The Subjectivity and Consciousness of Animals

I FALSE CONCEPTUAL ECONOMY

As we have seen, people have until lately placed the burden of proof somewhat oddly in approaching these topics. They have asked 'Is there any reason to believe in subjective states in animals?' as if subjectivity were a kind of phlogiston, an extravagant metaphysical hypothesis, and the negative answer to it were the safe, economical one. But in raising any such question, we need to start from the facts to be explained. We must therefore begin, 'Granted the similarities between nervous systems, and also between many of the ways in which animals interact and the ways in which humans do, and granted also that humans often interact with animals successfully, *how wide a difference in their basic social faculties does it make sense to posit?*' It is not economical to posit a greater difference between the causes than is needed to suit the difference in the effects. If we accept the arguments just given (and countless others like them) for agreeing that it makes sense to talk of subjective states in humans, and also to say that other humans can often roughly identify these states, reasons must be found for *refusing* to say the same about animals. The actual extent of successful interaction cannot be sneezed away. Every day and all around us, even in our urban and restricted way of living, people rightly assess the moods of dogs, and dogs of people. Cats, horses etc. are also doing very nicely. In the Amazonian jungle, where it really matters, they do better still. Any player in this game can of course make mistakes. But people can also do that about other people. The concepts which we successfully use here are a selection from those which we employ in thinking about the moods, feelings, perceptive powers etc. of human beings – concepts such as sight, alarm and anger. There is not an extra, abstract, general phenomenon called subjectivity or consciousness which would have to be separatedly detected and added as a kind of stuffing for some of the players. Subjectivity is an integral aspect of these terms. And the reason why the terms are used in the first place is not sentimental fancy. It is that they supply the only way in which we can even describe what happens intelligibly, let

134

alone explain it. As the psychologist O. H. Mowrer (while still struggling gamely to maintain a Behaviourist position) sadly remarked, 'if consciousness were not itself experienced, we would have to invent some such equivalent construct to take its place'.[1]

Attempts at purely external descriptions of behaviour, such as 'Head drops by 7 cm., ears by 3 cm., tail by 21 cm., fur on back contracts' etc. are never going to make sense to the listener, unless he receives a sudden flash of contraband enlightenment, leading him to exclaim: 'Oh I see – what you mean is that it's frightened. It is cowering because it has seen the predator.' After this flash, however, he is able to make all sorts of further useful predictions. He now 'knows what is happening'. His previous method forbade him ever to do so.

The ideal which has been thought to demand these odd ways of thinking is the Principle of Parsimony. This principle dictates that, of two explanations which explain equally well, we should choose the simpler one. It does not dictate that we should choose an explanation which does *not* explain rather than one which does. Nor does the more general tendency to deny that things exist necessarily make for simplicity. Cutting down the furniture of the universe with Occam's Razor is not a cure-all. (If it were, we might do better to settle for the phenomenalist's more thorough-going solution and eliminate independent physical objects altogether, or indeed adopt total scepticism.) Instead, the simplicity which we need is that of a conceptual scheme which *works* – which draws together the facts of experience so that we can interpret them consistently as a whole, and which is fertile in further relevant predictions. Since individual experience is extremely slight, transient and patchy, we need for this a good deal of standard conceptual scaffolding, a background system of assumptions stretching far beyond what any or all of us can check by direct sensations. This set of assumptions includes the continued existence of the physical world when we do not monitor it, and the general reliability of memory. It also requires the reliability – therefore the existence – of other intelligent witnesses. So it assumes the subjectivity or consciousness of other human beings. (A solipsist could not do science.)

These assumptions are not only compatible with our experience; they are necessary to make it possible. Scepticism about them is necessarily humbug. To talk, or even to think directedly, is to assume an ordered world in which we are not alone, and whose order is far too extensive and complex for us ever to have observed it all. Puritanical horror of such basic assumptions will not make our thinking more rigorous. It will simply destroy it. Parsimony or economy cannot be an absolute ideal. In thought as in life, the price which should be paid is relative to the value and necessity of the goods paid for.

2   CONSCIOUSNESS AND COMMUNICATION

In sum, the point of explanations is to explain. During the last few decades, Behaviouristic scepticism has been steadily losing ground as a general psychological creed, simply because in so many fields it vetoes usable explanations without providing better ones to replace them. It is barren. There are areas where it does no harm, because in them it happens that outside behaviour is relatively intelligible on its own, and the data from consciousness are relatively obscure, slight or unhelpful. But many central fields of psychology are not like this at all. In them, the habit of rejecting on principle all the most obvious sources of information has increasingly come to look eccentric. This is true in general of the whole study of motive and intention. And it is particularly true of communication, because that is a topic where explanations which do not take proper account of intention and the conscious life which surrounds it fail with peculiar resoundingness. Since Chomsky challenged Skinner's conception of 'verbal behaviour', that point has been increasingly plain about language.

This has an immediate effect for the animal scene. As it happens, the last half-century has seen a complete revolution in our understanding of animal motivation, and still more of animal communication. Virtually nothing used to be known of these matters – 'known', that is, in the sense of being scientifically accepted and studied. It is fair to say that, for the sciences, the topic has only been discovered in this century. The traditional knowledge which has always existed about it, and indeed even that painstakingly acquired by naturalists, had not been examined, criticized and used by the scientific community at large. In spite of Darwin's interest,[2] it was largely forgotten, ignored or even ignorantly denied, because it did not suit the intellectual fashions of the epoch. Early in this century, however, zoologists began to reverse this trend by seriously taking up the study of animal behaviour – ethology. They invented methods which formalized that study, methods which aimed to incorporate some of the skills inherited both from naturalists and from shepherds, hunters and the like, whose trained powers of observation have always been their livelihood, while adding modern scientific precautions against superstition and over-interpretation. In this work, they found it entirely natural and necessary to use the regular vocabulary already employed to describe human motive. This (as I have suggested) is not surprising, seeing that it had in any case been invented for use on animals as well as humans.

3 RITUAL SCEPTICISM

This vocabulary did not crack or prove unsuitable under the strain of more methodical observation. There was no need – as there was for instance in the case of chemistry – to invent an entire new set of words. Terms were redefined, and new ones were added, without breaking up the general scheme. But because the vocabulary did seem to imply consciousness, both ethologists themselves and their critics were uneasy. The Behaviouristic fashions of the day seemed likely to condemn the whole enterprise as unscientific. The father of modern ethology, Konrad Lorenz, whose philosophic grasp and insight are entirely exceptional, rejected the whole Behaviourist doctrine from the first as confused, and said firmly that there was no difficulty in talking – to the extent that the vocabulary required – about the subjectivity of animals.[3] Other ethologists, however, largely bowed to the Behaviourist ruling. Following Tinbergen's example, they were often able to do this without damaging their investigations, by using purely ritual means. A paragraph was inserted, usually at the start of a book, which explained that all the words used should be taken in a sense which referred only to behaviour; no illicit or contraband knowledge was being claimed. This purged the general conscience and allowed writers afterwards to proceed in detail very much as they would have done under a less oppressive intellectual church. Thus, to take a typical example, Tinbergen does not hesitate to write, in his delightful book on gulls, of the satisfaction he has always derived simply from watching

the snow-white birds soaring high up into the blue sky, and assuming, or rather knowing, that they were feeling just as happy as I was.[4]

Officially, however, he thinks this knowledge impossible:

Because subjective phenomena cannot be observed objectively in animals, it is idle either to claim or deny their existence . . . Hunger, like anger, fear and so forth, is a phenomenon which can be known only by introspection. When applied to another subject, especially one belonging to another species, it is merely a guess about the possible nature of the animal's subjective state.[5]

This argument, as we have noticed, must apply just as much to people as it does to other animals, and when applied to people, it reduces us to solipsism. (What could it be like to observe, objectively, another person's feeling of hunger?)

What Tinbergen means by these manifestoes is – as emerges from his further remarks – simply to caution us against a lazy reliance on guesses about particular subjective states, to insist on the importance of using all possible sources of information, and of distinguishing between them, and in particular to warn us against underestimating the foreign element in the experience of other species. He does not at all need the extreme sceptical rejection of *all* judgements on the subject which I have italicized. Because he does not need it he does not even notice it – something which very commonly happens when people cite general principles in which they take only a background interest. He has therefore no suspicion of the damage it would do to his whole enterprise if it were consistently carried through. It is in fact impossible to use words like *hunger, anger* or *fear*, without associating some distinct kind of subjective state with them. The range of states which might pass as suitable is often very wide, but it is not infinite. These words are incapable of a sense which excludes that element. Of course it is true that anger, hunger and the like can on occasions be unfelt or unconscious. But then, equally, bricks can sometimes be unseen or unfelt. That does not stop bricks being, in general, tangible and visible objects.

4   THE RETURN TO REALISM

In the last decade, not surprisingly, this kind of ritual doublethink about animal consciousness has been cracking open. When once rigid Behaviourist doctrines about people had begun to give way, the oddness of maintaining them for animals became more and more obvious – especially, of course, to people interested in evolution. But there was still a certain inertia. There are times when psychologists, like penguins, can be seen crowding to the edge of an intellectual ice-floe, hungry for the nutritious facts swimming about below, but hesitating to dive until somebody else has tried it and escaped being eaten. On such occasions several enterprising birds often seem to splash in almost simultaneously. I shall not try to judge who first managed it on this occasion, by ignoring the tabus and bringing back words like *consciousness, introspection, subjectivity, self-knowledge, mental imagery, sympathy, imagination* and *dream* into obviously reputable scientific use. However, Donald Griffin has certainly been one early and very productive diver. He surveys both the difficulties of Behaviourism and the earlier attempts to overcome them admirably. He shrewdly notes the ambiguities and variations in Behaviourist language between modest agnosticism about the details of consciousness and stark denial of its existence – variations which have served to conceal the real difficulties of the position. He aptly quotes from Daniel Yankelovitch:

> The first step is to measure whatever can be easily measured. This is OK as far as it goes. The second step is to disregard that which can't be measured or

to give it an arbitrary quantitative value. This is artificial and misleading. The third step is to presume that what can't be measured easily isn't very important. This is blindness. The fourth step is to say that what can't be easily measured really doesn't exist. This is suicide.[6]

Griffin points out the essential arbitrariness of the sceptical position when it is directed only to animals:

> It is actually no more anthropomorphic, strictly speaking, to postulate mental experiences in another species than to compare its bone structure, nervous system, or antibodies with our own . . . The prevailing view implies that only our species can have any sort of conscious awareness, or that, should animals have mental experiences, they must be identical with ours, since there can be no other kind. It is this conceit which is truly anthropomorphic.

He notes, and correctly exposes, the bizarre moral arguments with which this arbitrariness has sometimes been defended. For instance, M. J. Adler had argued that

> if it were to be established by some future investigations that animals differ from men only in degree and not radically in kind, we would then no longer have any moral basis for treating them differently from men, and, conversely, this knowledge would destroy our moral basis for holding that all men have basic rights and an individual dignity.

Griffin merely comments that, 'followed to its logical conclusion, this argument implies that the comparative investigation of communication behaviour has more dangerous potential consequences than nuclear physics had in the 1930s' and leaves this morbid terror of truth to discredit itself.

In this book I have repeatedly tried to deal more fully with the suspicions which underlie such arguments. Most of them, as it seems to me, only need to be held up to the light to lose their persuasiveness. But they have usually not been examined, and their effects in shedding darkness must not be underestimated.

To return to Griffin: He carefully examines the issue of parsimony, and shows how often hasty attempts to achieve it by scepticism have proved self-defeating:

> It may be helpful, and even parsimonious, to assume some limited degree of conscious awareness in animals, rather than postulating cumbersome chains of interacting reflexes and internal states of motivation. Behaviour patterns that are adaptive in the evolutionary biologist's sense may be reinforcing in the psychologist's terms, as well. Perhaps natural selection has also favoured the mental experiences accompanying adaptive behaviour.

5 EVOLUTION DEMANDS CONTINUITY

This last point is extremely powerful, because, for anybody who does not believe in the special creation of man, it not only may but *must* be true. People do have mental experiences; no psychologist any longer wants to deny this characteristic of our species. But if they do have these experiences, they have acquired the capacity for them in evolution. So it must have conveyed some advantages. What were they? Are they likely to have been ones which only became important at the stage where pre-human anthropoids gave way to humans? There are two uncommonly solid reasons against supposing so. The first is physiological. Nerves capable of transmitting consciousness would surely have to be enormously more subtle and powerful than nerves incapable of doing so. The greater we suppose the difference to be, the more it ought to show up in the structure of the nerves and their supportive system. Yet no such marked difference appears. Griffin notes the importance of this. He reasonably remarks that from the scientific point of view it is natural to suppose that

as mental experiences are directly linked to neurophysiological processes – or absolutely identical with them, according to the strict behaviourists – our best evidence by which to compare them across species stems from comparative neurology. To the extent that basic properties of neurons, synapses and neuroendocrine mechanisms are similar, we might expect to find comparably similar mental experiences. It is well known that basic neurophysiological functions are very similar indeed in all multicellular animals. On this basis, we might be justified in turning the original argument of the strict behaviourists completely upside down –

and should conclude that, whatever indescribable thing consciousness may be, it is the same everywhere. In fact, Voltaire's question remains: 'has nature arranged all the means of feeling in this animal, so that it may *not* feel?'

The other reason concerns function. What are the *uses* of consciousness? Tradition, following Descartes, has tied them closely to our higher intellectual capacities, particularly to logic, mathematics and speech. It is not, however, in the least plausible that these capacities could arise directly from a state of total unconsciousness. Nor is the evolutionary advantage to be derived from logic and mathematics on their own at all obvious. Speech may seem different. But speech only gains its point among creatures who are already social. Solitary beings could not use it. In fact, before any of these faculties can be used, those possessing them must already have all the very complex emotional and perceptual adaptations which make it possible to live harmoniously together. But no creature could even start on the arduous road that leads to this condition unless it was already conscious.

6 THE USEFULNESS OF THOUGHT

This point has been admirably argued by Nick Humphrey, another deep-diving pioneer psychological penguin. He points out that psychologists have for some time accepted the idea that the advantage of thought in general is to supply a 'mental model of reality'. This model enables a thinking being to deal with aspects of reality which have not actually turned up yet – to extend its power of response by imagination far beyond the narrow limits of what has already hit it, and so grasp wholes and anticipate emergencies. It has not, however, been noticed what this commits us to as soon as we consider animals which are social – which must interact together if they are to survive. Such animals need, not just to notice behaviour, but to attribute motives in order to interpret it. For this, they must rely on their own feeling. Again, it is necessary to realize how extremely scanty any individual's actual experience is. For instance, if each could only learn what threats mean by trial and error, and could only learn to take warning from the panic of others when he had many times found that it predicted disaster, most creatures would be dead before they were educated enough to start living. For social creatures, the behaviour of those around them is the main guide to survival. *But they can only use it if their powers enable them to understand it.* This requires imaginative interpretation. A threatened individual must not only see movements and hear noises; he must perceive anger. As Humphrey says,

> If a rat's knowledge of the behaviour of other rats were to be limited to everything which behaviourists have discovered about rats to date, the rat would show so little understanding of its fellows that it would bungle disastrously every social interaction it engaged in . . . And yet, as professional scientists, behaviourists have always had enormous advantages over an individual animal, being able to do controlled experiments etc. . . . An animal in nature has only its own experience to go on, its own memory to record it, and its own brief lifetime to acquire it . . . Nature's psychologists succeed where academic psychologists have failed, because the former make free use of introspection.[7]

This may well suggest a science-fiction story on the lines of *Vice Versa*, where a seasoned experimenter wakes up to find himself a rat, and one not too well up in the dominance order . . . How is he going to manage? Such thoughts are salutary.

Humphrey rams his point home by drawing attention to certain phenomena which would scarcely make any sense if animals were not conscious, but which make very good sense when considered as fields for developing their imaginative powers. The most striking are dreams, play and the apparently unnecessary social interactions which constantly go on, especially conflicts between parents and their offspring.

All these things can be seen as affording practice in emotional states which an individual has not yet experienced, but which he needs to get accustomed to, both in order to handle them better if he later does experience them himself in earnest, and to recognize and cope with them in others. In this way he becomes able to 'model' social situations which confront him, and to find ways of resolving them without disaster. For this modest purpose, it is not necessary to achieve anything like that exact likeness between subjective states which has obsessed the sceptics. A rough, functional parallel is perfectly adequate. As Humphrey says:

> It need make no difference at all whether the other animal is actually experiencing the feelings with which it is being credited; all that matters is that its behaviour should be understandable on the assumption that such feelings provide the reasons for its actions. Thus for all I know no man other than myself has ever experienced a feeling corresponding to my own feeling of hunger; the fact remains that the concept of hunger, derived from my own experience, helps me to understand other men's eating behaviour.

The evolution of consciousness in animals is a fascinating topic, which I would very much like to pursue further. But I have now made the point needed for the argument of this book. We have explored the notion of anthropomorphism in order to investigate the sceptical suggestion which it is often used to express – namely, that we can know nothing of conscious states outside our own species. On that view, 'anthropomorphizing' is a special, fallacious and misleading way of reasoning, displayed whenever people attribute either conscious experience in general or particular conscious states to animals. Its fault consists in the extrapolation of notions derived from human experience to apply to the non-human.

I have met this objection by pointing out that *all* our reasoning extrapolates from limited experience. There is nothing wrong with this in general. To show that it is wrong in particular cases, we need to show that the gap is actually too wide for the comparison to be valid. Neither in the case of God nor in that of other animals is it obvious that this must always be true.[8] Over animals, the attribution of emotions is not an extension built out from a language completely formed, but a way of thinking which certainly goes back beyond the formation of language, since non-human animals of different species can understand each other. Its justification is of the same kind as the justification of our beliefs about the inner states of other people – namely, its general success. The degree of mutual understanding which we have, both with our own species and with others, is only made possible by attributing moods, motives and so forth to them on the rough model of our own, and constantly correcting the resulting misunderstandings. In this sort of situation, scepticism itself makes absurd demands on our credulity. It is really not plausible to suggest that this degree of success is produced without any real understanding, entirely by luck.

13 What Can Matter to Us?

Most of this book has been occupied with a negative, with removing barriers which our tradition has erected against concern for animals. When those barriers are down, what follows?

I have said little about this so far, save to indicate that our concern can take many forms. In particular I have distinguished social concern, directed to conscious beings, from the wider, ecological kind, directed to all living things and perhaps too to the lifeless world which they inhabit. Within these two kinds, plainly, many sub-divisions can arise and many sorts of conflicts are possible. These I cannot deal with here. We can only glance, and that briefly, at the general principles which should guide us in deciding how widely, in general, concern ought to flow.

This problem can be looked at in two ways. One could be called the 'minimalist' view, and seems often to be connected, in the minds of those who favour it, with the intellectual Principle of Parsimony. It advises us to care for as few things as possible – to examine every candidate for our attention sharply, and to consider everything worthless which has not been positively proved to be to our advantage. As we have seen, this principle is not easily satisfied. Even inside our species-barrier, there is no social unit larger than the detached individual which can be guaranteed to resist its solvent force. Applied consistently, it reduces human life to a set of isolated, competing atoms. But this is no recipe for happiness, nor even for security. We must ask, what was the point of the minimalism in the first place?

The answer is, I think, the usual one, that it is an exaggeration of a perfectly sensible point. Prudence does often call on us to curtail our concern for a particular institution or set of people, sometimes because it is really misplaced, but often just because it is out of proportion to what is needed elsewhere. Our powers, which are genuinely limited, must not be wasted. And because it is hard to shift emotional habits, quite sharp destructive weapons are developed to make these changes. But these then tend to go on being used for their own sake on things which are not wasteful at all. Thus, the hostility to religion in a great deal of Greek and Enlightenment thinking has often been deserved, and has been directed against many errors and abuses. But it has also attacked a number of things of great value. Among them has been that sense of wonder, of awe at the vastness of Nature, and of humility at our own dependent and insignificant place in it, which we need if we are to function realistically as part of the biosphere where we belong.

It seems doubtful, then, whether minimalism can even be effective as a means to its own official aim, our individual safety. But supposing that it could, what about our fulfilment and happiness?

Human beings do not seem to be creatures designed for a firmly limited life. It is characteristic of them, even when they have security, to reach out beyond it, never to be satisfied, to be always curious and enterprising. The question how far they should reach is of course partly answered by prudence; there are sharp limits on what is possible. But within those limits no other obvious boundary appears. It is not true, as has often been suggested, that we cannot be interested in anything unlike ourselves. Both poetry and science show us being interested in all manner of unlike things, and the unlikeness itself is often the ground of interest.

And the principle of following that interest is the alternative to minimalism. It is the mainspring of science. Science is not just an intellectual game, carried on among a set of human players. It is a genuine attempt to explore the universe. Among the parts of that universe which are within our reach, the other animal species which share our planet with us are a most significant part. They are not just put there as a convenience for us, neither are they just an oppressed minority in human life. They are the group to which we belong. We are a small minority of them. It seems reasonable to suggest that we ought to take them seriously.

Certainly we have a choice in the matter. We can be minimalists if we like. What we usually do is to display a rather mixed and arbitrary set of choices, changing them only when their inconsistency becomes unbearably uncomfortable. The quickest way to relieve inconsistency is often to abandon some choice or other. And this is the policy which generates minimalism. But there are other possibilities.

When some portion of the biosphere is rather unpopular with the human race – a crocodile, a dandelion, a stony valley, a snowstorm, an odd-shaped flint – there are three sorts of human being who are particularly likely still to see point in it and befriend it. They are poets, scientists and children. Inside each of us, I suggest, representatives of all these groups may be found. The decision whether to go in for minimalism is the decision whether to suppress them or to take their advice. It is too large a problem for this book, and I must leave my readers to settle it.

Notes

1 Getting Animals in Focus

1 Spinoza, *Ethics*, Part IV, proposition 37, note 1.
2 Peter Singer, *Animal Liberation* (Jonathan Cape, 1976), p. 67.
3 Well discussed by John Passmore in *Man's Responsibility for Nature* (Duckworth, 1974), Chapter 2.
4 *Discourse on Method*, Part 5 (in *Philosophical Works of Descartes*, tr. Haldane and Ross, Vol. 1, pp. 115–18). See also two of his letters: to the Marquess of Newcastle (23 November 1646) and to Henry More (5 February 1649) in *Descartes, Philosophical Letters*, tr. and ed. Anthony Kenny (Oxford University Press, 1970), conveniently reprinted in *Animal Rights and Human Obligations*, ed. T. Regan and P. Singer (Prentice-Hall, 1976), along with much other useful material.
5 See Voltaire, *Philosophical Dictionary*, under 'Animals'.
6 This is also the central topic of my book *Heart and Mind: The Varieties of Moral Experience* (Harvester Press, 1981).
7 From *Five Years of a Hunter's Life in the Far Interior of South Africa* by R. Gordon Cummings (1850). Quoted in *Elephants*, by Richard Carrington (Chatto & Windus, 1958), p. 154.
8 See his *Lectures on Ethics* (tr. Louis Infield, Methuen, 1930), p. 239, lecture on 'Duties Towards Animals and Spirits'. We shall consider this view more fully later (pp. 51–2).

2 Competition is Real but Limited

1 The 'lifeboat ethic' of withholding aid from poor countries was proposed by Garrett Hardin in 'Living on a Lifeboat' in *Bioscience*, October 1974, and more fully in *The Limits of Altruism* (Bloomington, Indiana, 1977). Its meaning and status are well discussed by Peter Singer in his *Practical Ethics* (Cambridge University Press, 1979), Chapter 8; his notes supply further reading which will put this suggestion in perspective and also relate it to the claims of animals.
2 'Utilitarianism ... seems to simplify unduly our relations to our fellows. It says in effect that the only morally significant relation in which my neighbours stand to me is that of being possible beneficiaries by my action' (W. D. Ross, *The Right and the Good*, Oxford, 1930, p. 19).
3 This tendency to 'social atomism' is very well discussed by Elizabeth Wolgast in *Equality and the Rights of Women* (Cornell University Press, 1980). See

also my paper on 'The Limits of Individualism' in *How Humans Adapt: A Biocultural Odyssey* (Smithsonian Press, 1983).

4 *Republic*, Book 5, 462c.
5 For example Shulamith Firestone, *The Dialectic of Sex* (Jonathan Cape, 1971), p. 12.
6 p. 108.
7 'Plant foods yield about ten times as much protein per acre as meat does . . . The implications of all this for the world food situation are staggering. In late 1974, as a famine situation began to develop in India and Bangladesh . . . the Overseas Development Council estimated that if Americans were to reduce their meat consumption by only 10 per cent, it would free at least 12 million tons of grain for human consumption – or enough to feed 60 million people . . . Indeed if Americans were to stop eating grain-fed beef altogether the grain released would be enough to feed *all* the 600 million people of India' (Peter Singer, *Animal Liberation*, Jonathan Cape, 1976, p. 179).
8 See his Introduction to the *Study of Experimental Medicine* (tr. H. Capley Greene), pp. 99–105.
9 See for instance the articles in *Animals in Research: New Perspectives in Animal Experimentation*, ed. David Sperlinger (John Wiley & Sons, 1981; produced under the auspices of the RSPCA).
10 See Peter Singer, *Practical Ethics*, Chapter 8, and McNamara himself in the *Summary Proceedings* of the 1976 Annual Meeting of the World Bank/IFC/IDA, p. 14; also in the *World Development Report* 1978 issued by the World Bank (Washington, DC, 1978).

3 Emotion, Emotiveness and Sentimentality

1 Emotivist ethics may be found briefly expounded by A. J. Ayer in Chapter 6 of his early book *Language, Truth and Logic* (Gollancz, 1936; Penguin Books, 1971), and in a more considered form by C. L. Stevenson in *Ethics and Language* and *Facts and Values* (Yale University Press, 1945 and 1963). Criticisms of it are now extremely common; a good one is G. J. Warnock's in *Contemporary Moral Philosophy* (Macmillan, 1967), Chapter 3.
2 Article in the *Guardian*, 24 October 1979.
3 Discussion piece in *Science* 179, 18 May 1973.
4 Letter in *New Scientist*, 10 January 1980.
5 Richard Heims, former head of the CIA and sometime US Ambassador in Iran, in an interview, *Observer*, 9 December 1979.
6 The much more subtle relations which really do exist between morality and emotion are well discussed by Bernard Williams in his paper 'Morality and the Emotions', in *Morality and Moral Reasoning*, ed. Casey (Methuen, 1971), reprinted in his *Problems of the Self* (Cambridge University Press, 1973).
7 An admirable exposition of methods which make it possible to approach these awkward problems soundly and objectively can be found in *Animal Suffering: The Science of Animal Welfare* by Marian Stamp Dawkins (Chapman & Hall, 1980). She gives special attention to discovering the actual preferences of battery chickens.
8 See an article 'Loose Housed Calves Make a Cheaper Veal' in *The British*

Farmer and Stockbreeder for 12 April 1980. At that time Quantock Veal, the biggest veal producers in the UK, turned over to the method. For a fuller account, see *Ag. the Journal for Non-Violence in Agriculture*, no. 59, June 1980. For more information on the whole topic, see *Factory Farming, A Symposium*, ed. J. R. Bellerby (Education Services, London, 1970).

9 Kant, *Groundwork of the Metaphysic of Morals* (tr. H. J. Paton under the title of *The Moral Law*, Hutchinson, 1948, Chapter 2, pp. 80–81).

4 The Rationalist Tradition (1): Absolute Dismissal

1 In his essay 'Apology for Raimond Sebond'.
2 Remarks translated by Ben-Ami Scharfstein, p. 152 of his book *The Philosophers* (Blackwell, 1980). The source for the first is an early life by Colerus, Chapter 9, cited by J. Freudenthal, *Die Lebensgeschichte Spinozas* (Von Veit & Co., Leipzig, 1899), p. 62. The second comes from Spinoza's Letter 19, to Blythenburgh, 1665, *Correspondence of Spinoza*, tr. A. Wolf (Allen & Unwin, 1928).
3 See Spinoza's *Ethics*, part IV *Of Human Bondage*, Proposition 50, 'Pity, in a man who lives under the guidance of reason, is itself bad and useless', and its proof.
4 Translated by Scharfstein, *The Philosophers* (see note 2 above) from remarks of Leibniz's servant, reported in *Gottfried Wilhelm Freiherr von Leibniz* by G. E. Guhrauer (Breslau, 1846, reprinted Olms, Hildersheim, 1966).
5 Kant, *Lectures on Ethics* (tr. Louis Infield, Methuen, 1930), p. 240.
6 David Hume, *An Enquiry Concerning the Principles of Morals* (1777), § 152.
7 Hume, *A Treatise of Human Nature* (1739), Book III, part iii, section 1, *Enquiry Concerning the Principles of Morals* §§ 255, 82–5 and 188–90.
8 John Rawls, *A Theory of Justice* (Harvard University Press, 1971), p. 512; cf. p. 17.
9 John Passmore's book *Man's Responsibility for Nature* (Duckworth, 1974) was seminal here.
10 *The Merchant of Venice*, Act IV, Scene 1.
11 J. J. Rousseau, *Discourse on the Origin of Inequality*, in *The Social Contract and Discourses*, Everyman edn, Part 2, p. 225.
12 *Lectures on Ethics*, p. 239, 'Duties Towards Animals and Spirits'.
13 Arthur Schopenhauer, *On the Basis of Morality*, tr. E. F. J. Payne (Bobbs-Merrill, New York, 1965), §§ 8 and 19. These sections are reprinted in full in *Animal Rights and Human Obligations*, ed. T. Reagan and P. Singer (Prentice-Hall, 1976), pp. 124–8.

5 The Rationalist Tradition (2): Interests, Rights and Language

1 R. M. Hare, *Freedom and Reason* (Oxford, 1963), pp. 222–4.
2 Clarendon Press, 1980.
3 H. J. McCloskey, 'Rights', *Philosophical Quarterly*, 15 (1965), 115–27.
4 L. Wittgenstein, *Tractatus Logico-Philosophicus*, tr. D. Pears and B. F. McGuiness (Routledge & Kegan Paul, 1961), propositions 4.116 and 7.0.

5   *The Labyrinth of Language* (Mentor, 1968), p. 10.
6   Stuart Hampshire, *Thought and Action* (Chatto & Windus, 1959), p. 99.
7   L. Wittgenstein, *Philosophical Investigations*, tr. G. E. M. Anscombe (Blackwell, 1963), Part II, § i.
8   Sheila Hocken, *Emma and I* (Sphere Books, 1978), p. 63.
9   Muriel Beadle, *The Cat: History, Biology and Behaviour* (Collins and Harvill Press, 1977), chapter on 'Intelligence'.
10   See for instance Gilbert Ryle, *The Concept of Mind* (Hutchinson, 1949; Penguin Books, 1970), Chapter 4, on 'Emotion'.
11   Tr. Ronald Taylor (Harcourt Brace Jovanovich, 1973). This book shows admirably what a complex hierarchy of faculties is subsumed under the name 'animal intelligence', and how many of them are also present in man. If we want to understand what intelligence really is in man, we need to explore this whole range of faculties, which constitutes its ground floor.
12   I have discussed this point further in my *Beast and Man*, Chapter 10.
13   A point well treated by Stephen Clark, *The Moral Status of Animals*, pp. 22f. and 34ff. I have said some more about it myself in an article called 'Duties Concerning Islands', *Encounter* for February 1983, reprinted in *Environmental Philosophy: A Collection of Readings*, ed. R. Elliott and A. Gair (University of Queensland Press, 1983).
14   Controversies about 'talking apes' have been somewhat unfruitful in settling this question, because they have become bogged down in angry demarcation disputes about human uniqueness, instead of being used to illuminate the different, but comparable, faculties which the apes display. Eugene Linden's *Apes, Men and Language*, in its new edition updated to explain these controversies, is probably still the best source.
15   Preface to *Discourse on the Origin of Inequality*, in *The Social Contract and Discourses*, Everyman edn, p. 172. Italics mine.

6 Equality and Outer Darkness

1   *Animal Liberation* (Jonathan Cape, 1976) p. 9.
2   *The Moral Status of Animals* (Oxford, 1977), p. 34.
3   In 'Do Animals Have a Right to Liberty?', in *Animal Rights and Human Obligations*, ed. T. Reagan and P. Singer (Prentice-Hall, 1976).
4   The journal *Inquiry* devoted a whole issue to these discussions (*Inquiry* 22, 1979), and they have continued vigorously. A more recent survey may be found in *Animal Rights and Human Morality* by Bernard E. Rollin (Prometheus Books, New York, 1981).
5   For farm animals, a good source is still Ruth Harrison's *Animal Machines* (Stuart, 1964). Things have not changed very much. On animal experimentation, *Animals in Research* (ed. Sperlinger, John Wiley & Sons, 1980) gives an excellent survey of the facts and some good discussion. Singer's *Animal Liberation* also has good, brief, informative chapters on both topics.
6   *Leviathan*, Part I, Chapter 14.
7   *Social Contract*, Book I, Chapter 13.
8   *Émile*, Everyman edn (tr. Barbara Foxley), p. 10.
9   *Discourse on the Origin of Inequality*, Part I.

10   *Émile*, Book 5, Everyman edn, p. 437.
11   *Social Contract*, Book I, Chapters 2 and 6.
12   *Social Contract*, Book II, Chapter 1.
13   Orwell's story is, of course, so transparently a fable meant for human application that little attention is usually paid to its literal meaning. The opening of it is, however, very interesting in its direct literal sense. Orwell plainly knew a lot about conditions on farms, and the speech of Old Major the boar, which rouses the other creatures to revolt, deserves more attention than it gets. The ironies of the tale get an extra dimension here, which is certainly intentional.
14   See Germaine Greer, *The Female Eunuch* (Paladin, 1971), p. 301.
15   Herodotus, *History*, Book III, Chapter 80.

7 Women, Animals and Other Awkward Cases

1   *Émile*, Everyman edn, p. 322. The following quotations appear on pp. 330, 350, 325, 324 and 333–4; the last point is re-emphasized on pp. 344 and 359. For a fuller discussion of this whole issue and its startling effect in distorting political theory, see *Women in Western Political Thought* by Susan Möller Okin (Virago Press, 1980).
2   These quotations appear on pp. 328 and 339, 322, 340, 371, 373, 400, 326, 323, 370, 331, 339 and 424–5.
3   pp. 322 and 328.
4   3 Hansard CC1,888. Cited in 'Victorian Wives and Property' by Lee Holford, in *A Widening Sphere*, ed. Martha Vicinus (Methuen, 1980).
5   *Observer* Colour Supplement, 25 January 1981.
6   Both quotations are from C. G. Jung, *Psychology of the Unconscious*, tr. Beatrice M. Hinkle (Kegan Paul, 1946), pp. 112–13.
7   *Farmer and Stockbreeder*, 30 January 1962, quoted by Ruth Harrison, *Animal Machines* (Stuart, 1964), p. 50.
8   *Journal of the American Veterinary Medical Association* 147 (10), 15 November 1965. Quoted in *Animal Liberation* (Singer), p. 75.
9   *The Moral Status of Animals*, p. 9.
10   For a very interesting discussion of 'self-consciousness' in this connection, see *The Ape's Reflexion* by Adrian Desmond (Blond & Briggs, 1979). Desmond shows how this concept, which is often treated as a simple one, obviously applying only to man, has in fact many components, and how these can be found in varying degrees in various kinds of primate. He ends by showing the human form of it as indeed distinctive – but far less flatly and completely so than is commonly supposed.
11   *Leviathan*, Part 1, Chapter 14, Everyman edn, p. 71.
12   *Leviathan*, Part 2, Chapter 17, pp. 87, 88 and 89.
13   This is, of course, a central theme in Wittgenstein's *Philosophical Investigations*, correcting his earlier notion of language as consisting of propositions stating atomic facts. See particularly *Investigations*, Part 1, §§ 21–7.

8 Sentience and Social Claims

1　*Introduction to the Principles of Morals and Legislation* (1789), Chapter 17.
2　On the question of duties to non-sentient beings, see John Passmore, who finds them a considerable problem (*Man's Responsibility for Nature*, Part 2, Chapter 5, on 'Preservation'). Since he wrote, more attention has been paid to these matters, making good the neglect of an age possessed with social contract thinking, and picking up many useful ideas from earlier tradition. The idea of the biosphere as an organic whole within which we exist, and which so shapes our whole being that its other parts must concern us, was expressed by J. E. Lovelock in *Gaia* (Oxford University Press, 1979), and has had a wide influence. See too Timothy Sprigge, 'Metaphysics, Physicalism and Animal Rights' (*Inquiry* 22, 1979), for a philosophical argument of the need for such a notion, which is also discussed in several papers in *Environmental Philosophy*, ed. Elliott and Gair (Queensland Press, 1982). *Can Trees Have Standing? Towards Legal Rights for Natural Objects* by C. Stone (Avon Books, New York, 1975) considers the questions raised by various law-suits on such topics. It is shrewdly discussed by John Rodman, 'The Liberation of Nature' in *Inquiry* 22, 1979. Robin Attfield, in 'Christian Attitudes to Nature' (*Journal of the History of Ideas* 44, 1983) traces the sources of responsible stewardship in the Christian tradition, redressing some imbalance in Passmore's account. Stephen Clark surveys the whole issue well in Chapter 8 of *The Moral Status of Animals* and develops it further in a paper called 'Gaia and the Forms of Life' in Elliott's collection.
3　*Animal Liberation*, pp. 8 and 9.
4　John Rodman (see previous note) presses the first charge, R. G. Frey in *Interests and Rights* presses the second.
5　See p. 55 and note.
6　J. S. Mill, *Utilitarianism*, Everyman edn, p. 58.
7　See Kant, *Groundwork of the Metaphysic of Morals* (tr. Paton under the title of *The Moral Law*, Hutchinson, 1948), Chapter 2, pp. 90–93, on 'Persons', and pp. 66–7, on 'Respect or Reverence'.
8　A wider use of the term respect to cover 'respect for all life' was given currency by Albert Schweitzer (see Passmore, *Man's Responsibility for Nature*, pp. 122–3 and 202). In English, the word *reverence* may seem to render this idea better. Kant's German word *Achtung* covers both.
9　*Animal Liberation*, p. 21, my italics.

9 The Significance of Species

1　A point well dealt with by Bernard Williams in 'Persons, Character and Morality'. See his book *Moral Luck* (Cambridge University Press, 1981).
2　Cited by Marian Dawkins, *Animal Suffering*, p. 6, from T. Carding (1974), 'Work at the International Level for Animal Protection; *Animalia*, I, 3.
3　Introduction to *The Biology of Mental Defect* by Lionel Penrose (1949).
4　See Wittgenstein on the use of language for such things as 'asking, thanking, cursing, greeting, praying' (*Philosophical Investigations*, Part 1, § 23).
5　Jane van Lawick-Goodall, *In the Shadow of Man* (Collins, 1971), pp. 151–4 and 193–5. See also Adrian Desmond, *The Ape's Reflexion*, p. 217.

6   For cats see Muriel Beadle, *The Cat, its History, Biology and Behaviour* (Collins and Harvill Press, 1977), p. 85.
7   See Adrian Desmond *The Ape's Reflexion*, pp. 222–3, summarizing Jane Goodall's Leakey Memorial Lecture of 1978.
8   This situation is well described by Lorenz in Chapter VIII of *On Aggression* (Methuen, 1966) and distinguished sharply from true social behaviour. He calls it 'the anonymity of the flock'.
9   See Credo Mutwa, *My People, the Writings of a Zulu Witch-Doctor* (Penguin Books, 1977), p. 175.

10 The Mixed Community

1   Muriel Beadle, *The Cat, its History, Biology and Behaviour* (Collins and Harvill Press, 1977), p. 66.
2   Thomas Nagel, *Mortal Questions* (Cambridge, 1979), essay 12, on 'What Is It Like to Be a Bat?'.
3   See the very touching account of Polyphemus and his ram, *Odyssey IX*, 447–60. Polyphemus, it should be noticed, was not an outstandingly sentimental person.
4   Sheila Hocken, *Emma and I* (Sphere Books, 1978), p. 33.
5   II Samuel xii: 3.
6   For adoption by elephants, see Daphne Sheldrick, *The Tsavo Story* (Collins and Harvill Press, 1973).
7   See 'Play-Behaviour in Higher Primates, a Review' by Caroline Loizos, in *Primate Ethology*, ed. Desmond Morris (Weidenfeld & Nicolson, 1967).
8   The relation of play to the arts and other highly valued human activities has often been noticed. It is well treated in Johan Huizinga's classic book *Homo Ludens* (tr. the author and another, Paladin Books, 1970). I have dealt with it myself in a paper called 'The Game Game' (*Philosophy* 49, 1974), reprinted in abridged form in my *Heart and Mind* (Harvester Press, 1981).
9   I Corinthians xiii. 11.
10   *Games People Play* (Penguin Books, 1968), Chapter 1, pp. 23–4.
11   *In The Shadow of Man* (Collins, 1971), p. 202. Italics mine.
12   Collected by Passmore, *Man's Responsibility for Nature* Part 1, Chapter 2, 'Stewardship and Co-operation with Nature'.

11 What is Anthropomorphism?

1   Diels, *Fragmente der Vorsokratiker*, Xenophanes, fr. 15. See also frs. 14 and 16, and an interesting discussion in E. R. Dodds's *The Greeks and the Irrational* (Cambridge University Press, 1951), p. 181.
2   The philosophic importance of this enterprise is the theme of Gilbert Ryle's admirable book *The Concept of Mind*, which did a most useful job in separating it both from a mere methodological precept ('attend in psychology chiefly to the outside data') and from the strange metaphysical position that the data of consciousness do not really exist at all. Ryle saw that these data must be admitted as real, and as supplying an essential aspect of behaviour, complementary to the outside aspect observed by others. He retained, however, a strong bias, typical of Behaviourist thought, towards thinking

them *unimportant*, patchy and relatively unhelpful for the understanding of motivation. This bias remained for some time very powerful in linguistic philosophy, until its remarkable barrenness forced the development of a more balanced attitude.

12 The Subjectivity and Consciousness of Animals

1 Quoted by Donald Griffin, *The Question of Animal Awareness* (Rockefeller University Press, 1976), p. 49.
2 Shown particularly in his late work *On the Expression of the Emotions in Man and Animals* (1872), but present in all his writings.
3 See for instance *King Solomon's Ring* (tr. M. Kerr Wilson, Methuen, 1952), p. 152, and my own fuller discussion of this topic, *Beast and Man*, pp. 344–51 and 105–15.
4 *The Herring Gull's World* (Collins, 1965), p. xiii.
5 *The Study of Instinct* (Oxford, 1976), pp. 4–5.
6 *The Question of Animal Awareness* (Rockefeller University Press, 1976); this and the following quotations appear on pp. 56, 69, 46, 85 and 70.
7 In his article 'Nature's Psychologists', *New Scientist*, 29 June 1978, pp. 900–903, expanded in *Consciousness and the Physical World*, ed. B. D. Josephson and V. S. Ramachandran (Pergamon Press, 1979). See also Humphrey's article 'The Social Function of Intellect' in *Growing Points in Ethology*, ed. Bateson and Hinde (Cambridge University Press, 1976).
8 A very interesting discussion on this point in reference to God may be found in 'A Cognitive Theory of Religion' by Stewart Guthrie in *Current Anthropology*, Vol. 21 (no. 2), 1980, pp. 181–203. Guthrie (quite independently) develops my point about the legitimacy and inevitability of human modelling in religion.
It would be interesting to compare these two uses in more detail, and also to develop further the parallel possibilities about machines, which I have not considered here. I think them radically limited. Machines, since people make them, are already related to human thought in a much more direct and simple way; they do not contain the mysterious element of alien life. They really are, in all but their materials, expressions and reflections of human planning. They are therefore a weak and unhelpful parallel if we are trying to understand human relations to animals. Animals, in fact, are a unique case here in constituting a class of which we are really members. We are not, in any literal sense, gods or machines.

Index